Sounds

of

Celebration

Sounds

of

Celebration

John and Ruth Bell

Bridge-Logos *Publishers*

North Brunswick, NJ

All Scripture quotations and names are taken from the King James version of the Bible unless otherwise indicated.

Sounds of Celebration

Copyright © 1998
by John and Ruth Bell
Library of Congress Catalog Card Number: 98-72702
International Standard Book Number: 0-88270-756-6

Published by:

Bridge-Logos *Publishers*

1300 Airport Road, Suite E
North Brunswick, NJ 08902

DEDICATED TO those churches and leaders who thirst after God and who long to release their people into exciting, celebrant worship. We dedicate the principles of this book with a prayer that the same overflow of joy that we have experienced here in San Antonio, Texas, will be yours.

Contents

Foreword

It has been my privilege to know John and Ruth Bell for three decades. They are two of the choicest servants of the kingdom of God. Prior to returning to pastoring in San Antonio, they were outstanding missionaries in Japan. From the time I met them, there was within them a great love and desire for worship in the house of God. As they built the great church in San Antonio, it became marked by the "sounds of celebration"—which is the title of this book.

The *Sounds of Celebration* is a book that you will enjoy reading as it expresses what the Holy Spirit is saying and doing in the Church today John and Ruth Bell do not write from a theory, they write from experience. In their congregation they have found release through praise and worship and their lives have been changed. Your life will also be changed by the book you hold in your hands.

Throughout the world today, the incense of worship and praise is going up before our Father who is in heaven. Never was there a day when there has been a greater revelation of praise and worship as we find in this day.

I know every reader will be blessed as you read this book and use it as a teaching manual on the subject of praise and worship.

Dick Iverson
(Founder and Chairman of
Ministers' Fellowship International)
9200 N. E. Fremont Ave.
Portland, Oregon 97220

Introduction

Everyone loves a celebration! We celebrate the birth of a baby, we celebrate birthdays, weddings, Christmas, New Year, and so on.

Celebration time is an exciting time! It is a time when we try to look our best and give our best. A pastor whose church is experiencing a fresh visitation of praise stated, "Church should consist of a hilarious party, true purity, and God's power." The Lord commanded Israel to celebrate three times a year at the end of harvest. These were days of feasting, singing, and hilarious rejoicing. Israel's calendar centered on these celebrations.

Three times in a year shall all thy males appear
before the Lord thy God in the place which he shall

*choose; in the feast of unleavened bread, and in
the feast of weeks and in the feast of tabernacles.*

Deuteronomy 16:15

How much more we can celebrate today! Grace has
come to us without measure! Let us celebrate!

Ruth Bell

There has never been a time in the history of the
church, at least within our knowledge, when hilarious
celebration has swept God's people as today. Books and
sermons on praise, singing praises, and Scripture choruses
are everywhere. People ask what they can do to have this
exciting celebration in their church. With thanksgiving
we humbly share the principles that have revolutionized
our ministries. It is with this desire to bless you that we
present the following chapters.

John Bell

1

Celebrate with Praise and Worship

A new sound is sweeping the earth. It has swept into growing churches, with drums, guitars and keyboards. With it have come Scripture choruses that are replacing the songbooks popular for many generations. Young and old are caught up in it, transforming dullness into excitement. Churches once nearly dead are coming alive.

What is this sound? It is the sound of celebration—celebrating Jesus. Not just singing about Jesus—celebrating Jesus. Celebrating with exuberant, radical praise. Like a young couple expressing their love to each other without hesitation, this celebrant praise is without inhibition. The Church has rediscovered her first love, as she moves into the sounds of celebration.

***

I remember the excitement of my first date with John Bell. He had just graduated from Bible college, and I was a freshman. With special permission, he took me to dinner, after which we walked from East to West Tulsa, arm in arm.

We were madly in love. As we stood on the bridge that divides Tulsa, gazing at the lights and the river, Johnny turned to me and began to sing: "Let me call you sweetheart, I'm in love with you . . . " My heart beat for joy—it was a celebration.

***

The songs we sing and their focus affects our mood, our vision and our activity for God. Wars have been won by soldiers emboldened by a song. What would celebrations be without singing? God loves celebrations and He tells us in Psalm 100:1,2:

> *Make a joyful noise unto the LORD, all ye lands. Serve the LORD with gladness: come before his presence with singing.*

Our singing to Him is to be a joyful noise. Lively, celebrant singing lifts us into faith. Verse four of Psalm 100 outlines the three dimensions of true worship:

(1) Enter His gates with *thanksgiving;*

(2) enter His courts with *praise;*

(3) *bless* His name.

We must not forsake one dimension as we move into the next, like children laying aside old toys when they receive new ones. As praise refocuses us on the subject of our adoration, we move up into the next level, incorporating both the old and the new, which intensifies worship. A celebration is accelerated intensity.

Jesus tells us to ask, seek, and knock. Each of these actions is more labor-intensive than its predecessor. Asking can be strong or it can be weak. And usually when we seek something, we go after it intensely until we find it. Knocking is even stronger. Some people, when they knock on our door or ring the bell, sound impatient— "ring, ring, ring." It implies a spirit of persistence, and it brings our rapid response. This is accelerated intensity.

Coming into His presence with singing, we begin our worship on the level of thanksgiving which is "me-centered." Thanksgiving focuses on what He has done for us, celebrating our blessings. A life-style of thanksgiving is wonderful—it rules out worry, complaining, and strife. It is difficult to be negative and thankful at the same time. Thanksgiving eclipses the negatives.

From thanksgiving we rise to the "Him-centered" level of praise; our rejoicing is not for what He has done, but we praise Him for Himself. In praise we celebrate Who He is and all He stands for. Just as it is difficult to have a life-style of thankfulness and be negative, it is also impossible to overflow in consistent praises to the Lord without knowing that He reigns in all areas of our lives. Praise brings peace and confidence for both now and the future. It brings peace to relationships and creative solutions to life's problems.

Person-centered praise propels us toward the third level: that of blessing His name, with abandonment, adoration, and total surrender. At this point, the theme of our song often changes from "Him" to "You," bringing a fresh, new intimacy.

Worship on the thanksgiving level brings focus to ourselves and our blessings (things). This is what David calls entering the gates with thanksgiving. The gate was the first entrance into the Tabernacle of Moses (gates speak of access and authority), and just inside was the brazen altar of repentance—a picture of the Cross.

The salvation of the soul is reason enough to be forever thankful, and when we speak of worship on the thanksgiving level as "me-centered worship" it is not meant to downgrade it. Our worship must indeed begin there. The message here is that after beginning on the thanksgiving level, worship must rise to higher dimensions where Jesus is the focus and celebration centers on Him (His person).

It would be strange if someone whom you had taken to dinner kept thanking you for that meal over and over and continued to do so each time you met. However, it would be normal for him to say to someone, "My friend is a truly gracious host, he invited me for dinner and entertained me royally." At this point, thanksgiving has turned into praise, taking the emphasis from the gift to the giver.

Praise is the second dimension of worship. Psalm 100:4 says to "*enter his courts with praise.*" Throughout the Tabernacle all the furniture spoke of Jesus. Praise brings us to the next entrance in the Tabernacle plan—the curtain that leads into the Holy Place.

In praise, our worship is taken up with Him. We speak of this dimension as "Him-centered worship." We extol His glorious name and crown Him Lord of all: celebrating Him! The late Kathryn Kuhlman said: "If you have only ten minutes to pray, spend the first nine in praising Him."

The third dimension is yet another level. (Many things in Scripture come in threes.) We are told to bless His name, bringing us into God's presence with total abandonment, and entering through the veil into the Holy of holies. All personal agendas are forgotten. We center on Him alone, taking quality time; not allowing ourselves to be rushed by our own programs or plans.

It is on this level that we could possibly miss the supernatural. Most of us are frequently too busy for much time alone with God. Urgency grabs us here and there causing us to neglect the priority of His presence. Yet it is at this point that His awesome holiness and great power is manifested.

We used to sing "Take time to be holy"[1] without understanding what it really meant. The first two dimensions—thanksgiving and praise—will lead us into the third level of intimacy with God. At this level we are blessing Him, adoring Him and unreservedly abandoning ourselves to Him; celebrating Him without thought of time or people around us. This is the Holy of Holies experience.

In teaching the Pentateuch (the five books of Moses) at International Bible College, I was troubled over the three dimensions of the Tabernacle of Moses. Obviously the three areas of the Tabernacle picture our progressive spiritual experiences. If this is true, there should be three distinct experiences in our walk with God. I had only experienced two: salvation (typified by the outer court) and the Holy Spirit (symbolized in the Holy Place). Where and what was that third dimension? I asked myself.

When the emphasis of praise and worship came, I thought perhaps that was it, as praise lifts us out of ourselves into Him in a new way. I was not satisfied with this until my attention was drawn to three groups in the Bible who were anointed and noted what each of them stood for:

1. *The Leper* When he was cleansed, he was anointed with blood and oil on the right

ear (hearing the Word), right thumb (serving), and right big toe (walk). This cleansing of the leper speaks of salvation from sin, and it was a onetime occurrence.

2. *The Priest*: This was the anointing for ministry, the same as the above, on the right ear, thumb and toe. However, this was not a onetime anointing. In the Old Testament, the priests were anointed with oil every day. We also need that daily anointing as New Testament believer priests. This anointing stands for the Holy Spirit.

3. *The King*: Kings were anointed for reigning on the right ear, thumb and toe with blood and oil. This can picture the third dimension, and is the most powerful of all as it symbolizes authority, giving   you power over demons, disease and destruction.

I heard Benny Hinn say that the Outer Court is our place of salvation—most of us agree on this—and the Holy Place is our experience of the Holy Spirit. "But," he said, "if we want to move into the Holy of Holies, we must spend time in God's presence in the Holy Place, ministering to Him." He said whether or not we ever move into a ministry of the miraculous is dependent upon how much time we are willing to spend there (in the Holy Place).

When we first come to God in the Outer Court, it is to receive forgiveness and cleansing. But in the Holy Place we minister to Him, which helps thrust us into the third dimension of the Holy of Holies. That's the place of power— the place of God's awesome holiness where total obedience is required. (It is where the high priest of old fell dead if he had sin in his life.) Oswald Chambers said: "It takes me a long while to realize God has no respect for anything I bring Him. All He wants from me is unconditional surrender."[2]

The price for this place of power is total death to self, which comes through obedience and quality time in worship. It is willingness to put everything into His hands and let Him break it as He did the little boy's lunch that fed the 5,000. The breaking of the loaves and fish preceded their miraculous multiplication.

Death to self must be a daily experience. This ties in with the third dimension of worship—total adoration of the Lord, void of consciousness of others—just Jesus, with complete obedience both to the *logos* of the Word (the written Word) and the *rhema* (the now quickened Word). How would you worship if everyone were blind and only God could see you?

In Leviticus 1-3, the three voluntary offerings of Israel give a clear picture of these three dimensions of worship. Chapter three describes the Peace Offering, which is the Thanksgiving Offering. Chapter two presents the Meal Offering (also called the Meat Offering), which is a type of our Praise Offering to the Lord, and chapter one gives the details surrounding the Burnt Offering, a picture of total surrender.

When God describes something, whether it is the Tabernacle plan or these offerings in Leviticus, He starts with the highest (Himself) and works down. Thus, in chapter one, the Burnt Offering (the highest) is recorded, then the Meal Offering in chapter two, and the Peace Offering in chapter three. But from man's view, we start with chapter three, the Peace or Thanksgiving Offering, moving up to chapter two for the Meal or Praise Offering, and finally into His presence in chapter one, as we identify with the Burnt Offering—a giving of ourselves without reservation.

There are two important factors in these three offerings: First, they were voluntary and second, they were offered each time before the Lord at the door of the Tabernacle.

The phrase "before the Lord" is given repeatedly, showing that true worship is not form; is not unto men, but unto God; and is not to be inhibited by men. The higher one goes in this level of worship, the less aware he or she is of people. Third dimensional worship excludes the influence of others and centers only on Him: uninhibited celebration!

Each of the Levitical offerings was made "at the door of the Tabernacle before the priests," showing the importance of the local church for worship, and the importance of leaders and their involvement. These three offerings were also voluntary and were sweet savor offerings. How God loves the sweetness of our ascending praises when they come spontaneously from the whole heart.

The Meal or Praise Offering of Leviticus chapter two was made up of three elements: fine flour, oil, and frankincense. The fine flour speaks of God's Word (well-prepared and finely ground), the oil is the Holy Spirit's anointing and frankincense shows the ascending vapors of worship and prayer. Each of these offerings was to be seasoned with salt:

> *And every oblation of thy meat offering shalt thou season with salt; neither shalt thou suffer the salt of the covenant of thy God to be lacking from*

thy meat offering: with all thine offerings thou shalt offer salt.

Leviticus 2:13

Salt in this instance speaks of covenant. God is a God of covenant, desiring to pour out His blessings upon His covenantal people. But He despises anything false or pretentious. He cannot tolerate facades or hypocrisy. Stale worship (without the heart's participation) is an abomination to Him.

A covenant is a two-way promise that is eternal. God keeps His covenant forever and He yearns for His worshippers to do the same. The Bible repeats the phrase: "The Everlasting Covenant" again and again. This covenant is as unchanging and as absolute as His Word. Today He is raising up a generation of praisers who celebrate Him within covenant commitment.

The Burnt Offering represents the highest dimension of worship. In Leviticus chapter one, verses one through nine, there are many challenging principles of how we can reach this level:

1. The Burnt Offering was "of the herd" without blemish. (Ordinary people can reach this level.)

2. It was offered "before the Lord and the priests." (Every worshipper needs to be accountable to a pastor of God's choice.)

3. It was flayed, cut in pieces and laid "in order" on the wood on the altar. (Our flesh must be stripped and cut in pieces. The wood speaks of the human element and in all worship, God wants order.)

    4. Its "inwards" (heart) and "legs" (walk) were to be "washed with water" (the Word).

    5. The whole offering was to be "totally burnt to ashes" (total commitment—nothing left).

Ashes in the Bible speak of deliberate humility. It is indeed a high level of worship when one is willing to be reduced to ashes. When we are nothing but ashes, there is no recognition of who we are. There is no self-identity. It was as a Burnt Offering that Abraham offered Isaac.

"Oh God, please humble me" I used to pray. But Jesus never put people down. He lifted them up. Humility is something we do deliberately. We are told in James 4:10 to humble ourselves, and the Lord will lift us up. We are told to be clothed with humility. Having the heart of a servant and being clothed with humility is something we have to work on. It doesn't come easily, but its results are wonderful.

In Hezekiah's revival, when the Burnt Offering was made, it brought the Song of the Lord:

> *And when the burnt offering began, the song of the LORD began also with the trumpets, and with the instruments ordained by David.*
>
> 2 Chronicles 29:27

We are living in the day of "the song of the Lord," which is released as we flow into the third dimension of worship. It is the Burnt Offering experience producing the supernatural and the prophetic.

At this level one forgets others and, like a child, celebrates Jesus without inhibitions. Jesus taught unless we become as a child, we cannot enter the Kingdom. A child responds instantly with tears or laughter, regardless of who is around. He gets excited and jumps up and down. The "kingdom" is a magical and marvelous place.

I used to come into the Lord's presence with tears, crying, "Please help me." One day I read Psalm 100:2: *"Come before his presence with singing."* Even though I had been a Christian for years, I didn't know I should enter His presence with praise. When I learned to begin my prayer with a celebration of Jesus, prayer became a delight.

Entering His presence with singing cancels doubt and confusion. Changing our prayer style to God's pattern brings faith and expectancy.

Isaiah 54:1 begins with the word *"sing."* This verse describes a song sung in the midst of desolation and barrenness. It is singing when nothing is going right—when everything seems futile and empty. Singing moves us from the blah's into celebration. We begin with thanksgiving, move into praise, then bask in His presence with high worship. That's when the fun begins!

1. Tabernacle Hymns Number Four (Chicago, Illinois: Tabernacle Publishing Co., 1955), p. 298.

2. David McCasland, Oswald Chambers: *Abandoned to God* (Nashville, Tennessee: Thomas Nelson Publishers, 1993), p. 46.

2

Celebrate with Perfected Praise

Charlie was driving along IH 10 on his way to Fredericksburg, Texas, when he heard a hubcap roll off his wheel. He quickly stopped the car, jumped out and reached into the tall grass to retrieve the hubcap and immediately felt a sharp, stabbing pain in his hand. To his horror, he found a rattlesnake hanging from his forefinger. Try as hard as he might, he could not shake it off.

Praying as he ran, he grabbed a hammer from the front seat of his car. By pounding the snake to death he was finally able to get it off his finger. By now, however, the burning venom was beginning to course through his body. He knew he must act quickly. Charlie scrambled back into his car and made a U-turn across the median, heading back to San Antonio and the hospital. All the while, he sang praises to the Lord.

As he pulled into the emergency entrance, Charlie began to feel dizzy. He had to get help soon but he knew he mustn't run. He had heard that running speeds the poison to the heart even faster, bringing rapid death.

Slowly, calmly, with praises to God on his lips for bringing him this far, he walked into the emergency room. Just inside the door he collapsed and lay unconscious on the floor. A diligent nurse spotted the marks of the snake's fangs on Charlie's hand, and the emergency room crew was able to save him. God miraculously spared his life. Singing praises in the face of death had helped calm Charlie's spirit and keep him alive.

As the story goes in Matthew 21, when Jesus rode the donkey into Jerusalem, the crowd went wild, giving Him exuberant praise. But when He arrived in the city, He began to cast out all who sold and bought in the Temple. He upset the tables of the moneychangers and the seats of those who sold doves. Then He spoke these words: *"It is written, My house shall be called the house of prayer; but ye have made it a den of thieves"* (Matthew 21: 13). Let's continue at verse 14:

> *And the blind and the lame came to him in the temple; and he healed them.*
>
> *And when the chief priests and scribes saw the wonderful things that he did, and the children crying in the temple, and saying, Hosanna to the son of David; they were sore displeased,*
>
> *And said unto him, Hearest thou what these say? And Jesus saith unto them, Yea; have ye never read, Out of the mouth of babes and sucklings thou hast perfected praise?*

What had happened to our gentle Lord Jesus? The celebrant praises of the children had aroused the warrior in Him. So today, when we celebrate Him with perfected praise, the warrior spirit in us arises. Our Lord had expected to find people praying and praising God in His temple, instead, He found them buying and selling.

Does He feel that way today when He finds everything but prayer and praise in His house? It's ironic how few people will attend prayer services, but let the church throw a big dinner and here comes the crowd.

After Jesus drove out the offenders He healed the lame and the blind, and the children started a praise choir "Hosanna to the son of David." When confronted by the chief priests about this, Jesus quoted from Psalm 8:2: *"Have ye never read, Out of the mouth of babes and sucklings thou hast perfected praise?"*

There's a dynamic truth here. Though Jesus was quoting from Psalm 8:2, the actual wording is *"Out of the mouth of babes and sucklings hast thou ordained strength because of thine enemies, that thou mightest still the enemy and the avenger"* (author's emphasis).

Jesus said, *"Out of the mouth of babes and sucklings thou hast perfected praise,"* teaching by application that "strength" and "perfected praise" mean the same. A person whose life abounds in praising God will not be negative and critical but will have great spiritual strength.

Weaknesses dissipate in the presence of radical praise. Nowhere in Scripture are we told to be weak—"Be thou weak in the power of His might"?—it's just not there. But over and over God gives the mandate to be strong. Praise and joy bring strength.

Four important things happened in Matthew 21:12-16:

1. When Jesus cleansed the temple, He showed that His house is a house of ***purity.***

2. He declared his house is also a center for ***prayer.***

3. In healing the blind and lame, He showed that His house is a base for ***power.***

4. When the children cried, "Hosanna to the Son of David," He defended them, showing that His house must be a place of ***praise.***

What Jesus desires is perfected praise which brings strength to His people. Praise makes church exciting. It brings life, purpose and joy to every service, and a sense of expectancy. Psalm 65:1 says, *"Praise waiteth for thee, O God, in Zion."* He has chosen Zion for His dwelling. He said in Psalm 132:14, *"This is my rest forever; here will I dwell."* He lives in our praises (Psalm 22:3). What will make church exciting? Continuous, hilarious celebration. *"In thy presence is fullness of joy"* (Psalm 16:11).

God is worthy of more than token praise. He is seeking those who will fill His house with perfected praise. Congregational praise should be more than responding to the leader with "Praise the Lord," or standing and praising together for ten or twenty seconds. There should be times of extended praise: quality time given to minister to the Lord, making room for Him to minister to us. When a congregation gives time for ministering to God, it brings about a spirit of warfare.

Our gentle Jesus didn't often show His anger, but something was aroused in Him that day when the children cried *"Hosanna! Hosanna!"* And when He saw what was going on in the temple, the aroused warrior spirit came forth with vehemence. Their radical praise birthed a response in Him.

The principle of evaporation and precipitation shows this truth. Job 36:27 says, *"For he maketh small the drops of water: they pour down rain according to the vapour thereof."*

If we expect to receive the rains of spiritual blessings we must faithfully send up the vapors of praise to fill God's clouds. When we send up our praises, God's clouds get full, and when the clouds fill up, the blessings come down.

Another beautiful Scripture is Ecclesiastes 11:3a, *"If the clouds be full of rain, they empty themselves upon the earth."* Our responsibility is to impregnate the clouds of heaven by sending up our praises to God. He responds by emptying His clouds upon us, causing floods of blessing. It is the law of condensation. This doesn't only happen where we are, but the clouds that we form by our praises can also spill out on people down the street for whom we have been praying.

How do we move from spasmodic moments of praise to ministering to the Lord for longer periods? We've observed the importance of two elements: quality time, and singing praises.

When the church at Antioch *"ministered to the Lord"* (this takes quality time) and fasted, the Holy Ghost called Saul and Barnabas to their first missionary journey (Acts 13:1). Quality time spent in prayer and praise releases a spirit of celebration which brings with it the supernatural. God's voice is heard, and the vision for His work is increased.

Pastor Reg Layzell of Vancouver, Canada, one of the greatest of God's praisers, helped our church to enter into extended times of praise. In one service when he was teaching he asked the people to stand and lift their hands and their voices loud enough to hear themselves, and praise the Lord for five minutes. "And I'll keep the time," he said.

Have you ever tried praising God for five minutes without stopping? That was a long five minutes. People were surprised. It demonstrated how little time we actually give in praising the Lord. We have since known many times of thirty or forty minutes of continued praise, but in those days it was not common. Deliberate celebration brought the change. The psalmist said, *"I will bless the LORD at all times: his praise shall continually be in my mouth"* (Psalm 34:1). This is the only way praise can be perfected, by continuous, hilarious praise, and by giving it quality time.

Not only is it important to make time for extended praise, another important dimension is to sing our praises instead of just saying them. Psalm 100:2 says *"Come before his presence with singing."* Since singing is the highest form of worship, singing praises lifts us into a higher realm of celebration.

At the last supper, Jesus and the disciples sang a hymn before they left for the Mount of Olives (Matthew 26:30), and without doubt, this strengthened our Lord for the ordeal He was about to face. Singing is a tremendous tool for praise.

The Lord has given us the opportunity to introduce on several mission fields the concept of celebrating with "singing of praises." Some years ago in Mexico, our interpreter informed us that the people needed help in their worship. We had the joy of teaching them how to sing their hallelujahs rather than merely saying them. Sing "Hallelujah"—then a step higher—"Hallelujah"—one more step up—"Hallelujah"—then coming down the scale—"Praise ye the Lord." The people responded beautifully.

Now all across Mexico, people are singing praises and celebrating in worship. What a thrill to recently witness how the glory came down upon a pastors' conference there. This happened as in every service they gave quality time to celebrating Jesus. When we rush through worship, we miss God's presence and His ministering response.

This celebration is not limited to specific groups or denominations. It is happening all over the world wherever people are thirsting for more of God. Prayer is exciting when it is filled with vapors of praise and celebration. We are told to praise Him with our whole being and with understanding. Praise makes our praying more meaningful; it ushers us into God's presence and makes talking with Him easy and delightful. Let's take the time to praise Him.

In Psalm 146 through 150, each Psalm begins and ends with "*Praise ye the Lord.*" Psalm 146 begins with, "*While I live will I praise the LORD: I will sing praises unto my God while I have any being.*" Psalm 150 ends with, "*Let everything that hath breath praise the Lord.*"

As long as God gives us breath, let us abound in praises and celebration in our individual prayer life, with our family and with our church, filling His sanctuary with perfected praise.

3

Celebrate with Singing!

"Leonard she's dying!" Mother wailed, as Mary Anna rolled her eyes in death. As we went to bed that night, we children had prayed our usual childish prayer: "Thank you Lord that no one in our family has ever died." That was the last time we were to pray that way.

Mary Anna was a beautiful baby of fourteen months with big blue eyes and blond curls. She was the darling of the entire compound of the Ikoma Bible College in Japan,where my parents were missionaries. In recent months they'd begun having problems with some new students who had enrolled from Korea.

Pre-World War Japan was not the affluent country it is today. Frequently people came to the Christian Bible

College expecting a free meal. They felt that all foreigners were rich. Students had been demanding money.

One night, just as we finished our evening meal, I became conscious of the strangely tense atmosphere.Our parents told us children to go into the room with bars on the windows and stay there. Not long after, we noticed that our house was surrounded with these new students.

When the doctor finally came, he said that Mary Anna had apparently been poisoned: possibly with a cookie with rat poison in it. Before she died, her stomach swelled up and her eyes rolled back. Our mother were devastated.

At our family altar the next morning our parents tearfully told us that Mary Anna was now in heaven. We were grief-stricken, but daddy led us in a song of worship.

Soon after the funeral, I heard Mother going through the house, singing praises to the Lord. Her constant singing kept her from bitterness. Throughout the years that followed, Mother never expressed hatred for the Japanese or the Koreans, only a compassionate sorrow that so many in Japan were still without the gospel. Somehow, her song made it all right.

The first word in Isaiah 54 is "*sing!*" Verse one says: "*Sing, O barren, thou that didst not bear; break forth into singing, and cry aloud, thou that didst not travail with child.*"

Anyone can sing after the baby is born, but what about when the church seems dead and the worship seems lifeless? When there are no newborns, no children, no excitement, no wonder, no baby Christians, nor wild visions of the young; no radical issues to challenge the status quo and vision is dim? Nothing can wipe out a church and prevent exciting growth like deadness and apathy. And God says to sing?

When there is no reproduction and everything seems empty, that's when the *"sacrifice of praise"* produces power. The picture in Isaiah 54 was one of utter desolation, but the prophet cried out, *"Sing."* Sing, when things are disappointing, for with that singing, we release God's dynamics, and things begin to change. In verse two the prophet says: *"Enlarge the place of thy tent, . . . spare not, lengthen thy cords, and strengthen thy stakes."*

Celebrating God's praises, especially when things are bleak, enlarges us. When I face a problem, I go into our livingroom, kick off my shoes and dance before the Lord, putting the problem under my feet. Dancing in praise is like pushing Satan's crushed head further into the dust under us. This cancels thoughts of escapism—(Satan tempts us with the "escape syndrome"). Singing enables us to face the problem head-on with victory and authority. Singing activates verse three: *"For thou shalt break forth on the right hand and on the left"*—(true enlargement).

This moves us forward with expectation and faith, and rules out fear of failure. People who talk of escape or divorce are already thinking failure. Singing to the Lord in the face of difficulty rules out failure. It declares from your spirit: "Jesus is Lord, and He reigns." Verse four promises: *"Fear not; for thou shalt not be ashamed."*

In Isaiah 54, the prophet projects eight exciting results when we sing in the midst of desolation:

1. Though the mountains be removed, God's kindness remains (vs. 10)—[even in a great earthquake].

2. God's covenant of peace shall not be broken.

3. All your borders will be pleasant stones (vs. 12).

4. All your children shall be taught of the Lord (vs.13).

5. Great shall be the peace of your children.

6. You will be established in righteousness (vs. 14).

7. You will be far from oppression.

8. No weapon formed against you shall prosper (vss. 15-17).

If you feel spiritually barren and desolate, sing and celebrate Jesus. In Jeremiah 33:11, God promised to turn our captivity of discouragement and bring total restoration as at the first:

> *The voice of joy, and the voice of gladness, the voice of the bridegroom, and the voice of the bride, the voice of them that shall say, Praise the LORD of hosts: for the LORD is good; for his mercy endureth for ever: and of them that shall bring the sacrifice of praise into the house of the LORD. For I will cause to return the captivity of the land, as at the first, saith the LORD.*

In Hebrews 13:15, we are challenged: *"By him therefore let us offer the **sacrifice of praise** to God continually, that is, the fruit of our lips giving thanks to his name"* (author's emphasis).

When things are going well, praise comes easily and is no sacrifice. When God is blessing in a beautiful praise service and we are flowing together, it is easy to celebrate

Jesus. But it takes the *"sacrifice of praise"* when our world seems to fall apart, when circumstances go in reverse and we are the object of criticism and apparent failure. That's the time to *"SING, O barren . . . "* This is celebration!

"By him therefore let us offer the sacrifice of praise to God continually, that is, the fruit of our lips giving thanks to his name" (Hebrews 13:15).

Acts 16:26 tells us that when Paul and Silas were in jail, they began singing. Their legs and arms in stocks, the jail doubtless was damp, dark, and smelly, with rodents running wild. It may have been a sacrificial praise, but it worked. God shook everything with His earthquake, and they were set free. So it is with us. The unusual happens when we give a sacrifice of praise in the face of obstacles.

Singing praises is repeatedly commanded in scripture. Psalm 47 says, *"O clap your hands, all ye people; shout unto God with the voice of triumph."* Verse five describes the ascension of Jesus and the next two verses tell us what we are to do until He returns to reign over the heathen:

Sing praises to God, sing praises: sing praises unto our King, sing praises.

For God is the King of all the earth: sing ye praises with understanding.

Five times in the above verses we are told to sing our praises. As a girl, I was taught to say my praises to God, but in recent years we've been enriched by being taught to sing our praises in celebration. Singing is the highest form of worship. And when we celebrate, we always need a song. So let the sounds of celebration ring out!

Not only does singing praises lift our spirit, but musical instruments used to glorify the Lord add another dimension in praise. Psalm 98:5, 6 declares:

> *Sing unto the LORD with the harp; with the harp, and the voice of a psalm.*
>
> *With trumpets and sound of cornet make a joyful noise before the LORD, the King.*

Musical instruments are mentioned in many other scriptures, some of which are Psalm 150, 2 Chronicles 5:13, and Revelation 18:22. Celebrate with musical instruments!

Another dimension in singing praises to the Lord is in the new song birthed by the Holy Spirit. Psalm 96:1 commands: *"O sing unto the LORD a new song."* Some "new songs" are only for the moment while others continue to bless the whole church.

Moses was used of the Lord to write many beautiful songs. Exodus 15 records the song he sang after their great deliverance from Egypt. Israel had just come out of a lengthy enslavement—over 400 years. Unlike many "soul" songs today, Moses' song had very little in it of self-pity or "me-centeredness." Perhaps if we had been writing it, we might have wailed about the woes of slavery and the sufferings of the past. What were the words to Moses' song in verses 1 and 2?

> *I will sing unto the LORD, for he hath triumphed gloriously: the horse and his rider hath he thrown into the sea.*
>
> *The LORD is my strength and song, and he is become my salvation: he is my God, and I will prepare him an habitation; my father's God, and I will exalt him.* [A celebration!].

Again, just before his death, after leading Israel for forty years, God told Moses, *"Write ye this song for you, and teach it the children of Israel: put it in their mouths"*(Deuteronomy 31:19). Turn to Deuteronomy 32 and read this last song of Moses, and let the Holy Spirit lift you up in worship as its words magnify God's faithfulness and His greatness. There's not a hint of bitterness in Moses' song, nor a hint of his disappointment over not going into Canaan. The entire song is a celebration of the Lord.

Have you been singing new songs to God? Psalm 149:1 tells us to *"Sing unto the LORD a new song."* God dislikes staleness. In the wilderness, He operated by the "something new" on a daily basis. Fresh manna was given each day, right from the sky, except for the double portion each weekend in order to keep the Sabbath. If anything should have a fresh new touch, it should be our worship. Even cattle need new pasture in which to feed, otherwise, their feet become diseased. Sing a new song unto the Lord!

Hannah sang a new song to the Lord after she left Samuel at the temple (1 Samuel 2:1-10). Mary sang the Magnificat (Luke 1:46) before the birth of Jesus. In Revelation 14:3, they sang *"the song of Moses the servant of God, and the song of the Lamb, saying, Great and marvellous are thy works, Lord God Almighty; just and true are thy ways, thou King of saints."*

There is a touching testimony of a pastor in New Zealand whose wife gave birth to twins. To his utter grief, a few hours after birth, one twin died and then the other. He couldn't understand it, and began to question God. Then his wife died, leaving him devastated. The days passed, and his anguish was unbearable. He was unable to sleep at night and walked the floor weeping. This went on for weeks. He felt he couldn't go on living. He had no inspiration for preaching or preparing sermons—just unending questions: "Why? Why?" He seriously considered leaving the ministry. Night after night he walked the floor crying out, "God, why did you take my wife? It was bad enough to lose the twins, but I can't continue in the ministry without my wife."

One night as he was sobbing, he opened the Bible at random to Psalm 30:11 and with tears pouring like a river read: *"Thou hast turned for me my mourning into dancing: thou hast put off my sackcloth, and girded me with gladness."*

At that instant, God put a tune into his spirit, and he began to sing it, dancing and celebrating before the Lord. Out of his grief a beautiful new song was born as he put melody to the Scripture. This song has circled the globe and with it, his testimony. As he sang that night, the pastor was released from his sorrow, and he is today happily serving the Lord.

Sing! O barren, Sing! Celebrate the Lord with singing.

4

Celebrate by Agreeing with The Word

Elaine was nervous anyway, driving in heavy traffic on the Freeway. But when three year old Lisa in the back seat said, "Mama, there's a snake crawling on the back of your seat" her heart began to pound, and she felt her hair beginning to stand on end.

How was she to handle this one? She and Lisa had just been memorizing Luke 10:19:

Behold, I give unto you power to tread on serpents and scorpions, and over all the power of the enemy: and nothing shall by any means hurt you.

Very softly and calmly she told her daughter not to make any noise or sudden moves, but to sit back quietly and watch God work for them, according to the verse they had just learned. In a quiet voice she began to command the snake to crawl across her shoulder toward her window, which she was slowly opening, and to crawl down her arm and fall onto the pavement below. Between her commands to the snake, she softly sang praises to God, keeping her mind on Him, and not allowing herself even one negative thought.

To her amazement, she could feel the snake across the back of her neck, slowly moving toward the open window, and down her arm. When it reached her hand, she said, "In the name of Jesus!" and shook it off into the street. This is a true testimony. Agreeing with God's Word as the basis of our praise brings miracles. When we move by the Word instead of by our feelings all of heaven's power is released on our behalf. God's Word always brings victory.

"Where are these Scripture choruses coming from?" the question is often asked. All over the world it is happening. Psalms and verses of Scripture are being put into melody from Japan to Australia and from Mexico to Africa. Why is this? Our bridegroom has an Eleazer out there busily preparing His Rebecca for the wedding. They are the sounds of celebration.

God is not coming back for a weak, pimple faced, teenage bride who moves by feelings or the weather, with moods swinging from deep depression to hilarious joy. He is coming back not only for a rejoicing bride, He is returning for one who is efficient, well-equipped, healthy, beautiful, glowing, and strong.

Too long the church has moved in the realm of feeling. Too long we thought we were saved because we felt like it, were healed because we felt better, were victorious because we felt good. We know that feelings follow, but it is faith that brings the miracle, and praise raises our faith level.

Someone asked a Christian who was trusting God, "How do you feel?" The Christian's answer was, "My faith is in His Word. My feelings have nothing to do with it. " Agreeing with God's Word is more than simply giving assent to it. Len Jones says: "Christianity is not a *think so* or even a *believe so* thing. It is the great confession—the great *say so* thing."[1]

I heard Kenneth Hagin say that God never does anything until He first says it. When we speak God's Word, we activate its power. In Genesis 1:1 God created the heavens and the earth. In verse two His Spirit moved upon the face of the waters. But in verse three, God said something. When God spoke, His Word brought forth creative forces. Today, miracles are happening all over the world as God's Word is spoken in faith by His believing people.

Nowhere in Scripture are we admonished to be weak. But over and over we are commanded to be strong in the Lord and in the power of His might. We are told in Nehemiah that the "*joy of the Lord*" is our strength. The singing of the Scriptures enables us to memorize them. This is good, as it quickens the Word to us. Our son Nathan frequently asks the question when he first sees someone: "How's your joy today?" He receives some interesting answers.

Joy, strength, and the Word are linked together. To move into higher dimensions of praise, it is vital that we learn to agree with God's Word. This is the opposite to how we are conditioned. Our world lives by its feelings. Hunger tells us to eat; when we're hot we turn on the air conditioning; when we're cold we turn up the furnace.

Rhymes and ditties tell us to take this for a headache, take that for an upset stomach. The television shouts to us, "Smell it, touch it, hear it, see it!" The next time you watch a TV commercial, notice where it is directed—right to your senses. We are doubtless living in the most sensual days in history. And in the middle of it all, a new rhema is sounding through the land: "Agree with the Word! Agree with the Word! Disagree with your feelings and agree with the Word!"

Do you need healing? God has not required that you feel healed. All He asks is that you "Agree with the Word." Then what does the Word say? *"By whose* [Jesus'] *stripes ye were healed"* (1 Peter 2:24, author's insertion).

Agree with what God's Word says, not with how you feel or how things appear or what the doctors say. God's Word will outlive all those other words. It will outlive the universe. It will outlive your senses. It will outlive and outpower the words of the physician. His Word will win. It is up to us to verbalize it—speak it out loud. Let the demons hear you quote it.

Bless the LORD, O my soul, and forget not all his benefits:

Who forgiveth all thine iniquities; who healeth all thy diseases.

Psalm 103:2,3

Verbalize your praises to God in quoting these Scriptures. Agree with His Word by your praises. That is not being hypocritical. It is not lying.

There is a pastor and his wife in our city whom we love to hear pray. We have been with them in many kinds of difficult circumstances, yet always, when they pray, they praise God for the solution, and never dwell on the problem. Prayer that praises God in the midst of a trial is a celebration of God's greatness and faithfulness.

Get with your husband or wife, or your son or daughter. Get with someone on your job or in your church. Sing and say your praises aloud together and agree with God's Word as you celebrate His promises. Jesus said in Matthew 18:19:

> *Again I say unto you, That if two of you shall agree on earth as touching any thing that they shall ask, it shall be done for them of my Father which is in heaven.*

"Anything . . ." Jesus said that if we agree on anything we shall ask, it shall be done of the Father. Begin now to praise God as you agree with His Word, not the circumstance, not the negatives, not your doubts. Agree with His Word! David said in Psalm 138:2:

> *I will worship toward thy holy temple, and praise thy name for thy lovingkindness and for thy truth: for thou hast magnified thy word above all thy name.*

As powerful as God's name is, David said His Word is magnified even above His name. Just as Jesus zonked Satan with the Word of God after His forty days of fasting, we have a gold mine of untapped resources in His Word.

Agreeing with the Word works even in the awesome face of death. The woman in Elisha's day who lost her son by sunstroke saw a great miracle through her ability to agree with the Word of God and function by faith.

The boy had been helping his dad in the field when he ran to him crying, "My head, my head!" When they carried him to his mother, she took him upon her knees and there he died (see 2 Kings 4:20). Nothing is more final or more fearful than death. And yet, not letting fear's doubts overwhelm her, she laid him on the prophet's bed (in the little chamber they had built for Elisha), and ran in search of him. As she was leaving she called out to her husband in faith, *"It shall be well."*

Can you imagine saying such a thing with your child lying dead? When Elisha saw her coming, he sent his servant to meet her. The servant asked, *"Is it well with thee? is it well with thy husband? is it well with the child? And she answered, It is well."*

This is not some weird story of a mother without feeling for her son. She was evidently in deep anguish from the way she fell at Elisha's feet and said, *"As the LORD liveth, and as thy soul liveth, I will not leave thee."* The Bible says Elisha arose and followed her. She was agreeing with the Word of God for healing for her boy, even for a resurrection.

2 Kings 4:32 says that when Elisha came to the house, he found the child dead. Here was a mother faced with the finality of death itself, yet she so agreed with God's promises, she closed herself off from doubt and demanded the prophet come and activate God's Word. She agreed with the Word, not the circumstances, and her boy was raised back to life. Do we say in distress, doubt, and discouragement, "It shall be well—It is well?"

Look at God's perspective. He sees you in a difficult position—even in a dark valley. He hears you praising Him, celebrating His Word, thanking Him that "It shall be well." How does this affect His great compassionate heart? The one element that God responds to above all others is faith. Praising God in agreement with His Word is the key to this kind of faith. Agreeing with God's Word brings you into a new dimension of praise, and interestingly, praise brings you into a new dimension of faith.

I have a dear friend who had cancer of the breast, and after a mastectomy, went through chemotherapy. It made her very ill and she lost her hair, but she never lost her confession. Like the mother in 2 Kings, no matter how difficult it was, she always answered "It is well."

She said this so often to her doctor he finally asked her what it meant. She shared with him the account from the Bible. He saw it worked such miracles for her, he had her speak to his other patients in their difficult times. That's been nine years ago now, and she can still say "It is well!"

When Dwight Eisenhower was a boy, he was dying with gangrene of the leg. His fever was raging, and the doctor said the only way he could save him was to amputate the leg. Before he lost consciousness, Dwight made his brother, Edgar, promise to stand in the way of the doctors, and not allow this to happen.

His parents, who were of the Red River sect of the Mennonites, were deeply religious, and they prayed for him morning and night. They were agreeing with God's Word which they read together as a family after every meal. The next morning Dwight's fever broke, the infection was better, and the crisis had passed—all because they celebrated the Word of God in faith.[2]

Agreeing with God's Word stabilizes us and lifts our faith above our feelings. When this is done with praises, it accomplishes two things: it helps us feel a whole lot better, and it causes the dynamics of our faith to release God's miraculous power on our behalf. Our sounds of celebration penetrate the problem bringing us into God's victory when they are based upon our agreeing with His Word.

1.Jones, Len; *Confess It!* (Dorchester, Dorset, England: Mission, 1946), p.1.

2. David, Lester and Irene; *Ike and Mamie: The Story of the General and His Lady* (New York, N.Y.: G.P. Putnam's Sons, 1981), pp. 43, 46. Eisenhower, Dwight D.; *In Review: Pictures I've Kept* (Garden City, N.Y.: Doubleday & Co., Inc., 1969) p.8.

5

Celebrate His Lordship In Every Situation

"For He is Lord of lords, and King of kings " (Revelation 17:14). The phrase "Jesus is Lord" has become popular in recent years, especially in evangelical circles. The chorus "Jesus is Lord" was one of the fastest to sweep the world and has been translated into many languages.

With the current emphasis on praise and worship, churches are getting away from "me centered" songs, knowing they do not bring a blessing that lasts. The thrust today is to turn the emphasis away from ourselves and toward the lordship of Christ. There are seminars, women's clubs, men's fellowships, music symposiums and various groups who are teaching key principles on how to be celebrant worshippers. In many places leaders are no longer called "song leaders" but rather "worship leaders" or "worship teams."

Our generation doesn't need "poor me songs." People don't need to be reminded of their confusion, failures, and hurts. They get enough of that in their families and work places. When they come to church they need solutions and Bible answers. Their focus needs to be redirected from themselves to the Lord.

Frustrations and disappointments are sometimes of our own making—from doing our own selfish thing, and from failing to let the Holy Spirit be our leader and our wisdom. But how do we attain the right focus? How do we get away from that "self" who creates confusion? How do we really make Jesus our Lord of everything?

It is one thing to sing "Jesus is Lord" at church, while beautiful worship ascends to God's throne. It is easy then to feel He is totally Lord of all, but how is it when we are out on the job, faced with everyday difficulties? How is it when we are misjudged or falsely accused, or are underpaid, or rejected at the moment of an anticipated promotion? It is at these times, in the midst of negatives, that a truly new dimension of praise can be our experience, by celebrating Jesus as Lord of everything.

A dedicated pastor and his wife were ministering for a week in a city where their ex-daughter-in-law and their two grandchildren lived. On their first night there, they had called to ask if they could see their grandchildren, and had received a cold refusal.

All week long, without telling others about it, they ministered to the convention while their own hearts were breaking. On their final day, early in the morning, the pastor's wife awakened to her husband dancing before the Lord, thanking Him. Though it was hard, he was going to bless the Lord and praise Him for every situation just as it was. His wife lay in bed chuckling at the sight of her husband dancing in his pajamas.

At that moment the phone rang. It was the ex-daughter-in-law: "Dad, you can have the children today all day if you wish. I kept them out of school so they can have a nice long visit with you." What had changed her? The previous communication had been one of curt refusal. What had happened to make her change her mind? The pastor had made Jesus Lord even in the face of a crushing circumstance, by celebrating Him.

Praise in the midst of negative circumstances does not come easily. But it is not difficult when you base it on God's Word, and set your will to deliberately rejoice in His lordship. It comes through a revelation of Christ's reigning power now.

I was blessed with a beautiful mentor in my childhood, my older sister Faith. She helped take care of us five children while mother was busy with the ministry in Japan. When we received a phone call from Dallas saying that Faith's husband, Pastor Wally Denton, had suddenly passed away, we hopped a plane and rushed to her side, intending to comfort and strengthen her in her hour of grief.

Instead, we found Faith standing at her front door comforting and praying with the people of the church who were weeping in her arms. She stood there like a queen, receiving all kinds of people and ministering strength to them with the words: "The Lord reigns." Though she was in grief also, there was a special strength that undergirded her emotions. That strength was her focus on the lordship of Jesus, and it enabled her to sing and smile even when her heart was breaking.

Why did God send the fiery snakes to bite and destroy His people in the wilderness? Because they murmured.

Why does God hate murmuring? Because He knows that the minute a Christian murmurs—the moment he complains, criticizes or practices self-pity, Jesus is not lord in his responses. The moment a Christian permits indulgence in negatives, self has displaced Jesus from the throne, and replaced Him with pride and self-pity.

There is a misunderstanding among many that as long as gossip is not public, or as long as complaining or criticism is done in private, maybe just to one very close individual, it can be reclassified as something else, and therefore is not sin. This is deception.

Negative talk is the opposite to praise, and will hinder prayer, praise, and faith. It will stifle your spiritual growth, and prevent you from celebrating the Lord. Husbands and wives must especially be on guard here. Opinions that would never be breathed to another soul are frequently aired in intimate relationships, and could delay for years God's anointing, either in you or in your companion. God said of Israel in Psalm 106:24,25: *They believed not his word: But murmured in their tents* [in their homes]" (author's insertion).

Don't be party to Satan's deception by sharing your self-pity with your husband or wife. Resist the devil and he will flee. Squash that impulse to say that negative word. Instead, begin to praise God, and celebrate your faith. Bless the Lord out loud, even if you don't enjoy the sermon or when the car falls apart, or in the face of illness or financial stress.

Make Jesus lord by verbalizing your praises "in your tent." It is often in the home where these victories are won with lasting results. Our home is our base from which all other activities spring. If we win the victory there, it is easier to praise God in the midst of the larger crisis out in the world. Celebrate God in your home.

In Proverbs 6:16-19 God lists six things which He hates, and the seventh one which He abhors—*"sowing discord among the brethren."* Usually that's what negative talk does. It brings discord and destroys celebration and praise. Disunity is one of Satan's favorite tools to hinder revival.

Another important principle is refusing to make comparisons. Children should never be compared with each other, or with neighbors' children. How often has your child said, "Well, everyone is doing it," using that as a lever for getting his way? Children are adept at this, and unless parents know the Scriptural admonition not to compare—2 Corinthians 10:12—they fall easy prey to this "everyone is doing it" syndrome.

Ministers often become discouraged by this, comparing another man's ability or ministry with his own or another man's congregation or facility. What does comparing do? It takes the focus off Christ and brings it back to us. Comparing is the forerunner of doubt. The moment comparisons are made, the Lord is no longer in our focus, and Jesus is not lord.

Blame or credit is now given to circumstances, talent, geography, personality, or age. This makes room for discouragement or pride, cancels celebration and causes the vision of Jesus as lord to be lost in the haze. How wise is God's Word! Don't compare, for this is not wise. Without God's Word as our measure, we quickly come into a fog of relativity which leads to deception. The Word will always center us back to Jesus making Him our focus.

It is exciting how in recent years many songs have been written about Christ reigning as king: "The Lord Reigneth," "Our God Reigns," and others. What do these songs tell us? That He is lord in every situation.

Employment agencies note that 90% of job changes are not due to inefficiency or a lack of skill, but rather from a buildup of personal resentment, usually connected with authority or the chain of command. Most irritations on the job are centered in personal offenses or pride. The wise man said, *"Only by pride cometh contention"* (Proverbs 13:10).

Here again, Christ has been displaced from the throne of our lives, and self has begun to reign. We think a job change will be the answer, but our pride goes along with us, and in a few months, a similar problem surfaces. What is the solution? How can a person who continues to change jobs break the pattern? By celebrating Jesus even within the difficulty.

The same principle applies to marriage. Those who have been divorced several times can usually find a pattern, if they look for it. And that pattern is often one of negative talk, discouragement through murmuring and criticizing, comparing one's self with the other, and cutting each other down. This pattern can be broken by making Jesus lord through praise, and celebrating His lordship and His reign.

Christianity is sometimes labeled an "escape from reality." It is just the opposite. Christ reigning in the nitty gritty of life is what enables us to stay on top of pressures and irritations. The important word here is "deliberate." When we deliberately set our will to praise Him in every situation, regardless, this generates His miracle power.

When circumstances are negative, through our praises we enable Him to reign in us now, in this life. When He is reigning in us, we are able to reign over our circumstances. True peace is not running away from a problem, for its roots will go with us, but true peace is getting above the problem by making Jesus lord over it. As we make Jesus lord in all things, He enables us to rise above them and look down on them as He does. This is not just celebrating God when we feel like it. It is also celebrating Him when we don't feel like it.

My favorite place in our home to face a problem is the living room. I go there and dance and celebrate on top of the negatives, declaring Jesus is lord over all. Many answers to prayer have resulted. As we celebrate Him when things look bad, we grind the crushed head of the devil further into the ground, under our feet, declaring in faith, that Jesus is lord of everything. Send forth the sounds of celebration as you make Jesus lord of all.

6

Celebrate and Change Circumstances

"We will have to operate immediately," said the doctor as he stepped over to his desk to call the hospital. "You are losing your life blood, and delay could be dangerous." He was not a man given to panic, but he made it clear that this was a case for immediate action.

Five minutes earlier, she had been weak and trembling and could barely write her name for the nurse. But now, in the face of the frightening verdict, a miraculous praise to God welled up within her. She could hardly believe what she was doing, as she sat up on the examining table and boldly declared, "And what if I refuse?"

The doctor shook his head in disbelief, explaining how risky it was to put it off. Amazed at herself, the patient continued to talk about recovery without surgery, that God would come through, that between God and her healthy cells, she believed she could get well without it. The doctor continued to shake his head, warning her of the danger. When she insisted on returning home, he said she should go to bed and would be unable to continue teaching.

That night the family prayed together. They entered into a faith-pact of praise, celebrating Christ's lordship and His greatness. The following three days the doctor, deeply concerned, made inquiry concerning the patient. Each day, it was with great delight that a positive report was given.

By the fourth day, the problem was completely gone, and she was back teaching. No surgery was needed. How did this happen? When praise welled up, it brought with it a surge of faith. Praise is one of God's greatest tools for releasing His miracles.

> *But thou art holy, O thou that inhabitest the praises of Israel.*
>
> (Psalm 22:3)

In a recent building program, it became necessary to obtain a bank loan for our church, but with the current economic situation, each bank rejected our request. Several months went by and it began to appear that the building project would come to a standstill. An unfinished building would not glorify Christ so we began to pray.

One morning before breakfast, we were praying about the building, when suddenly our prayers became praises. We began to celebrate Jesus, and a spirit of joy lifted us above the impossibility of our situation. Faith bubbled up, and my husband went to his banker again, and without thinking, he took from his pocket some pictures of the folks working on the new building, and showed them to him.

Excitedly, the banker asked if he could borrow the pictures to show to his board which was meeting that afternoon. That very day what had been only refusals before, turned into solutions, and we were able to obtain the needed loan to complete the building. Celebrant praise had released God's dynamic power to change our circumstances.

A biblical example of this is King Jehoshaphat's choir, which by simply celebrating God, defeated the armies of three kings who came against them. 2 Chronicles 20 tells the story. We have outlined it under three headings:

1. Jehoshaphat's Prayer

2. Jehaziel's Prophecy

3. Judah's Praise.

The besieged king set his face to seek the Lord and called all Judah to prayer. As they stood before God, with their children and their babies, a young prophet named Jehaziel began to prophesy that the enemy would be defeated. Then King Jehoshaphat took a step of faith and did a marvelous thing—he organized a choir:

> *He appointed singers unto the LORD, and that should praise the beauty of holiness, as they went out before the army, and to say, Praise the LORD; for his mercy endureth for ever.*
>
> *And when they began to sing and to praise, the LORD set ambushments against the children*

of Ammon, Moab, and mount Seir, which were come against Judah; and they were smitten.

Psalm 149:6-9 shows that the high praises of God in our mouth, and the two-edged sword (the Word of God) in our hand causes us to triumph over our enemies just as Jehoshaphat did.

Along with the "high praises" there are three other types of praise mentioned in Psalm 149 which God is emphasizing today:

1. Singing our Praises—even singing aloud in bed.

2. The New Song

3. The Dance

My mother used to tell us how that in the early 1900's when the outpouring of the Holy Spirit was fresh, it was common for people everywhere to sing their praises to the Lord. In the flow of these sung praises it was not unusual for new songs to be born in the congregation. Today we are in the thrust of a revival of restoration, not only the singing of praises and the new song, but also praising God in the dance.

When I was a little girl on the mission field, I would watch with envy when someone became drunk in the Spirit and danced in God's presence. We were taught that worldly dancing was wrong, but I used to stand there thinking how neat it must be to be that filled with the Holy Spirit, that you could dance "in the spirit" as it was called then.

But I never had that experience, possibly because I felt unworthy and never opened up myself to it. In recent years we learned from Psalms 149 and 150 that we are told to praise God in the dance. King David danced hilariously before the Lord, and when Michal, his wife, scorned him, she became barren.

When we saw this, we realized that the phrase "dancing in the spirit" was not a biblical term, and put a limit on God's people from praising Him in the dance. It is not said of King David that he "danced in the Spirit" but that he "danced before the Lord" (2 Samuel 6:14). The correct term then, is "before the Lord." Whether we are celebrating God by singing our praises, or with a new song, or in dancing, it is imperative that it be "before the Lord," a wholehearted celebration of Jesus.

Praising God in these three ways is a powerful tool in our hands by which God enables us to celebrate Him and change our situations. Try it.

When you were a child, did you ever have to wash the dishes? We did. And frequently, when we had company, it seemed like they were stacked like mountains, sticky and yucky, and hard to get clean. But even as children, experience brought us understanding. When we would sing as we worked, the dishes were done in nearly no time, and it became a fun experience. I remember my brother David and I harmonizing at the top of our lungs while we washed, rinsed and dried and put them away. Singing actually made the chore become fun. We were unconsciously celebrating the Lord.

God wants His high praises in our mouths and His two-edged sword in our hands so we can see circumstances change. The next time you are driving your car alone, sing His praises out loud. Let a new song come forth from your heart. Tomorrow before breakfast, try dancing before the Lord, and watch God change your trying situation into a tremendous triumph.

49

In 1958, we dedicated a small new church to the Lord in Ishikiri, Japan. Prior to this, there had never been a church in that town. We had begun with a tent meeting in which sixty-five young people were saved. It was a time of abounding joy and love. For months the new believers had been praying for a church building. Ishikiri is a town given to idolatry. Its economy is built on the Buddhist temple that sells pickled, poisonous snakes for the healing of skin disorders.

Not only did we teach the new believers the importance of prayer, we began to teach them about the dynamics of God's power that is released when we celebrate Him with praise in the face of impossibilities. When we united our praises with our prayers for a church building, suddenly the impossible turned into a miracle before our eyes.

One day our doorbell rang, and there on his red bicycle was the telegraph boy. He had in his hand a telegram from America that read: "One thousand dollars on the way for the new Ishikiri Church." The building took more than that of course, but from that small beginning, our faith rose as we celebrated Jesus, and the church was soon completed.

In that same year, the building of the new Fuse Church began. The situation was somewhat different, and the cost was a lot more, but again, faith was the answer. In this case, we had contracted with the builder to make a payment every three weeks. The new church was located about ten blocks from the Fuse train station.

Again miracles came through praise. Each time we walked those muddy roads through the rain, a celebrant praise bubbled in our hearts as we gave the builder his money. God was never a minute late. We knew we were out on a limb, for we had nothing left after we made a payment, and had no idea where it would come from three weeks later when the next amount was due. Some of those times we didn't even have food money left, but we never went hungry as God was always faithful.

Though it took everything we had to make the payment, three weeks later we found ourselves walking back to the Fuse station with another song of praise welling up inside. That song of praise from within was like a wheel of faith turning in our hearts. It was faith we could feel. It was faith that promised us that the next three weeks would see the need met again. It was a sense of celebrating God's faithfulness, and the church was completed debt free. But that feeling of victory was not there at the beginning. It came with deliberately celebrating God, when there was no human help in sight.

Celebrate Jesus even when you don't want to, and watch for your coming miracle that will change your circumstances.

7

Celebrate with Music

There's a sound of celebration throughout the land, especially in churches where free, hilarious worship is taking place. Many of the hymns and songs I grew up with are seldom heard. How my flesh loved the old hymns, but as God dealt with me about celebrating Him, I began to see how "me centered" some of them were. I loved some of them only because of the tune and the rhythm, or sometimes, merely because of the sentimental memory attached to them.

In some cases, their words had nothing to do with worshiping God but were very "me centered." All of this was more in the realm of sentiment than worship. When I realized this, a new appreciation came for the Scripture choruses that focus only on Jesus, His greatness and His faithfulness.

Music is one of God's greatest tools for bringing about "ascending worship" and thus producing unity and cleansing among His people. I once heard a Korean minister say that every child in North Korea is taught a musical instrument with which to worship the North Korean president. The whole nation of Israel was musical. And the purpose of their music was for worshiping Jehovah-God.

When Israel went into captivity in Babylon, their music ceased:

> *By the rivers of Babylon, there we sat down, yea, we wept, when we remembered Zion.*
>
> *We hanged our harps upon the willows in the midst thereof.*
>
> *For there they that carried us away captive required of us a song; and they that wasted us required of us mirth, saying, Sing us one of the songs of Zion.*
>
> *How shall we sing the Lord's song in a strange land?*
>
> (Psalm 137:1-4)

God's people knew that the purpose for music was to worship and adore their God, and this is difficult in a strange land under bondage.

King David gave a beautiful prophetic song in Psalm 126:1-3:

> *When the LORD turned again the captivity of Zion, we were like them that dream.*

> *Then was our mouth filled with laughter, and our tongue with singing: then said they among the heathen, The LORD hath done great things for them.*
>
> *The LORD hath done great things for us; whereof we are glad.*

Every mother should see to it that her children are taught music. But also, every mother should make sure that each child is taught the real purpose for music—that it is a tool for worship, and is reserved for worship of God alone. When our children are taught music, and they learn a musical instrument on which to celebrate and worship God, and are taught the importance of using music for Him alone, music takes on real significance. Psalm 149:1,2 says:

> *Sing unto the LORD a new song, and his praise in the congregation of saints.*
>
> *Let Israel rejoice in him that made him: let the children of Zion be joyful in their King.*

There are five elements of music that Satan is trying to destroy:

1. The **words** (Most important when directed to God)

2. The **melody** (Paul said, *"Making melody in your heart to the Lord"* Ephesians 5:19)

3. The **harmony** (Satan emphasizes unresolved tensions)

4. The *rhythm* (The world has emphasized rhythm beyond all else—a rhythm like the human pulse when ill with fever)

5. The *spirit of the music* (We should ask "What does it say? What spirit is it expressing?" (See James 3:15.)

Much of current worldly music has replaced the five essential elements listed above, with five other elements:

1. Immorality

2. Rebellion

3. Drugs

4. Perversion

5. Demon Worship

These themes in worldly music sometimes drive young people into depression and suicide. There's a reason for this. Satan was the main worship leader before he was cast out of heaven. He was uniquely created to be a leader among musicians and into his being were created all manner of jewels and musical instruments. Ezekiel 28:13-15:

> *Thou hast been in Eden the garden of God; every precious stone was thy covering, the sardius, topaz, and the diamond, the beryl, the onyx, and the jasper, the sapphire, the emerald, and the carbuncle, and gold: the workmanship of thy tabrets and of thy pipes was prepared in thee in the day that thou wast created.*

*Thou art the anointed cherub that covereth;
and I have set thee so: thou wast upon the holy
mountain of God; thou hast walked up and down
in the midst of the stones of fire.*

*Thou wast perfect in thy ways from the day
that thou wast created, till iniquity was found in
thee.*

It is ironic that Satan had ten different stones for his covering, showing that he was a creature of beauty and glistening colors, as well as a creature from which emanated music of various kinds. Rock concerts today emphasize lights and color, as well as noise and rhythm. There are seven principal colors in the rainbow, caused by clouds in the air, and music is a form of light, and there are seven principal notes in every scale. Jesus said: *"Take heed therefore that the light which is in thee be not darkness"* (Luke 11:35).

Music can lead either to "Lamb Worship" (Jesus the Lamb of God), or to "Beast Worship" (Satan). In Revelation 14:1,2 we are given a picture of Lamb Worship with new songs sung with harps by those who follow the Lamb *"whithersoever He goeth."* They are the redeemed. In Revelation 13:4, a picture is given of beast worship, as they worship the dragon who gave power to the beast. Verse eight says: *"All that dwell upon the earth shall worship him, whose names are not written in the book of life of the Lamb."*

Some people try to mix the two. Mixtures all through Scripture are known as one of the devil's favorite tools for deception. This is shown in Revelation 13:11: *"And I beheld another beast coming up out of the earth; and he had two horns like a lamb, and he spake as a dragon."*

This beast looked like a lamb, but spoke as a dragon. This is what happens when Christians try to mix music with a worldly thrust with the sacred. It is why we need to look beyond the surface and find the true message of the music. Someone has said: "The men who control the music of a nation control which god that nation will serve."

Recently I was sharing with a musician about my struggle as a teenager with worldly music. "What do you call 'worldly music?'" When I came to America at age fourteen, my friends at school wanted me to play popular songs on the piano for them to sing at lunchtimes like "Roll Out the Barrel," "Two Loves Have I" etc. Each time I played them, the Holy Spirit convicted me, until one day I gave my hands and talents to God.

To answer the above question, true music is inspired by God and enables us to glorify Him. This is God's ideal, and fulfills the real purpose for music. Worldly music is often sad; is about losing a lover, or about divorces, or love-triangles, and brings hopelessness and depression. Music for special occasions, patriotic songs etc., are inspired by man; but what we need to avoid like a snake is the music inspired by Satan, such as was used in Daniel 3:7 for worshiping the image. This music brings self-doubt, immorality and may even lead to suicide in some cases.

Since music is one of God's finest tools for bringing us into high worship, it is also a mighty tool to help us gain ascendency over our soul (mind, emotions, and will). Notice how music was used in Scripture:

1. To restore the true worship of Jehovah.

   A. When King Hezekiah came to the throne, he opened and repaired the temple gates and "set" the musicians in their places (2 Chronicles 29:25).

B. At the dedication of the second temple, Ezra "set" the musicians in their places to help restore true worship (Nehemiah 12:27,46).

2. To restore the soul (Psalm 23:3;57:6-11)

3. For meditation (Psalm 1:2) Singing the Scriptures

4. To affect the will—(Psalm 108:1-3) *"I will sing! I will awake! I will praise!"*

5. For teaching—*"Teaching one another in psalms and hymns "* (Colossians 3:1).

6. To reveal Christ's character (Ephesians 5:19-21).

7. To bring unity (2 Chronicles 29:27,28).

8. To bring healing and health—when David played the harp Saul was healed (1 Samuel 16:23).

9. To release God's miraculous power

10. To prepare His people for battle: trumpet warnings (Numbers 10:9).

11. To lead people into His presence (Psalm 22:3).

12. To release His prophetic Word—the prophet said, *"Bring me a minstrel"* (2 Kings 3:15).

An interesting story is given in 1 Kings 12 concerning the split in the nation of Israel after Solomon's death, when his son Rehoboam refused the compassionate advise of his father's counselors and decided to increase the national tax burden. One of his father's former servants, Jeroboam, led a revolt, and the nation's twelve tribes split with two tribes staying with Rehoboam (the royal line) and ten tribes going with Jeroboam.

To maintain cohesion in the nation, as well as reminders of God's faithfulness, the Lord had established three national celebrations when everyone came to feast and to worship Jehovah. To prevent the ten tribes from participating in this celebration at Jerusalem, Jeroboam built two calves of gold and set them up in Bethel and Dan, copying the religious system of the ungodly. Since he used Jehovah's name and the same order of worship, there was music involved. But he *"made priests of the lowest of the people, which were not of the sons of Levi"* (1 Kings 12:31). His music and system of worship were not under the authority of the House of God in Jerusalem.

Ultimately, all music should end up in the House of God. But Jeroboam's spirit of revolt brought in wrong worship, wrong priesthood, and wrong doctrine. The three go together and eventually lead to destruction.

Our music and worship on earth should be patterned after the worship in heaven. In Revelation 4 God's throne was the focus of the whole universe, and in verse 8 the living creatures were at the throne crying day and night, *"Holy, holy, holy, Lord God Almighty, which was, and is, and is to come."*

Each of these living creatures had a different form: one was like a lion, one like a calf, one like a man, and one like an eagle. Some believe this projects the various styles of worship leaders, for it was when these creatures gave glory, honor and thanks to the One on the throne, that the twenty-four elders fell down before the Lord, and cast their crowns before Him in worship (verses 9, 10). It is interesting to categorize worship leaders:

1. The Lion-leader is war like, choosing songs on spiritual warfare and victory.

2. The Calf-leader is joyful, often skipping and dancing in worship like a calf.

3. The Man-leader leads with compassion for people's needs.

4. The Eagle-leader, ethereal and mystical, is filled with awe as he leads ever upward into ascending worship.

Regardless of the leader's personality or form, every worship leader must remember that all music has one purpose, and that is to produce ascending worship, focusing on the Lord as the almighty, awesome God.

The creatures of Revelation 4:6 had eyes before, behind, and within, which tells us that worship leaders must have spiritual foresight (goals), and hindsight (learning from the past), and eyes within (insight into what God desires for that particular service).

Their wings speak of their ability to lift the worship to a higher level, and their perpetual crying *"Holy, holy, holy"* (4:8) speaks of instant response and continuity, plus a tremendous revelation of God's holiness, holiness that has no room for pride or competition or self-exultation.

In Revelation 5:14 they monitored the worship. They heard all creation praising God, and were pleased with what they heard. A good worship leader "measures" the worship and finds God's heart for that particular service.

Today God is restoring His music and His praise and worship to the church, fulfilling Jeremiah's prophecy in Jeremiah 33:10a,11:

> *Again there shall be heard in this place . . .*
> *The voice of joy, and the voice of gladness, the voice of the bridegroom, and the voice of the bride, the voice of them that shall say, Praise the LORD of hosts: for the LORD is good; for his mercy endureth for ever: and of them that shall bring the sacrifice of praise into the house of the LORD. For I will cause to return the captivity of the land, as at the first, saith the LORD.*

Just as Israel was known as a nation of musicians and singers, even so today, God's people are becoming known as musicians and worshipers. The churches that refuse this joyful, celebrant worship are also described in Revelation 18:21-24:

> *And the voice of harpers, and musicians, and of pipers, and trumpeters, shall be heard no more at all in thee; and no craftsman, of whatsoever craft he be, shall be found any more in thee; and the sound of a millstone shall be heard no more at all in thee;*
> *. . . and the voice of the bridegroom and of the bride shall be heard no more at all in thee.*

Craftsmen are known as specialists in a particular field, and are evident in the five-fold ministry of Ephesians 4:11, as are also other ministries, such as youth pastors, educators, and worship leaders. The millstone is for grinding out fresh meal —the fresh Word from the Lord when the fresh flow of the Holy Spirit is moving. When there is no fresh flow, there is also no sound of the millstone grinding out new messages with which to feed the sheep. God is never monotonous or dull, and it is important that we keep moving forward with Him in His fresh flow. Nowhere is this more important than in our music and celebrations of praise.

One of the most beautiful ways of keeping your music fresh is to encourage your musicians and singers to seek the Lord for new songs birthed in them by the Holy Spirit. We are challenged over and over in Scripture to *"Sing unto the Lord a new song"* (Psalm 33:3; 98:1; Revelation 5:9) But a new song can only be birthed in your spirit when you focus totally on Jesus, and forget about the inhibitions you might have in the presence of others.

Total focus on God is vital if worship is to continue with a fresh flow. Below are some principles for maintaining God's fresh anointing on your music:

1. Make the ministry (pastor etc.) a vital part of worship.

2. Change the concept of the worship service from ministering unto people to ministering to God.

3. Teach the eternality of worship; that worship is the essence of life, and is eternal.

4. Teach that we are all priests (1 Peter 2:5,9).

5. Change the concept of the choir/orchestra from performance to ministry unto God.

6. Charge your musicians to wait on God for a fresh expression of the Spirit.

7. Encourage strong, expressive celebrant worship and make time for it.

8. Require total unity in all areas, especially among the leaders and the instruments. Become a symphony unto the Lord.

9. Seek God until you know where He is leading, then share your vision, and move toward it.

10. Be a radical worshiper yourself, and encourage others to be also.

Celebrate! Adore Him! Abandon yourself to Him in enthusiastic praise and worship. Expect revelation to come. It usually comes through these progressions:

a. Celebration - (Exuberant praise).

b. Adoration - (High worship).

c. Revelation - (God will speak).

What a tremendous and miraculous force music becomes when it is only to exalt the name of the Lord.

8

Celebration Brings Authority

There is more space given to praise in Scripture than any other subject except one, and that is righteousness. Just as hostility and cursing strengthen all that is evil, praising God cleanses and reinforces all that is good.

Until recently, much of the church has been unaware of the dynamic powers that are released by praise and celebration. Paul E. Billheimer says:

The church at large should sincerely repent of its failure to comprehend the overwhelming content of the Word on praise, and render thanks to God for those instrumental in its rediscovery.[1]

Why is praise important? Because man was created for authority, and all authority originates with God. God's plan from the beginning was that His people take authority over all evil. God said in Genesis 1:26:

Let us make man in our image, after our likeness: and let them have dominion over the fish of the sea, and over the fowl of the air, and over the cattle, and over all the earth, and over every creeping thing that creepeth upon the earth.

Again in verse 28, God said to Adam and Eve: *"Replenish the earth, and subdue it: and have dominion."* David reiterated this in Psalm 8:4-6:

What is man, that thou art mindful of him?

For thou hast . . . crowned him with glory and honour.

Thou madest him to have dominion over the works of thy hands; thou hast put all things under his feet:

Praise helps us remember who we are in God, and that His original plan was for us to take authority and dominion.

A minister preaching special meetings in a small country community desired to get alone to pray, and went out into a nearby meadow. While praying, he heard a noise and looked up to see a wild bull charging toward him.

There was nowhere to go, no tree to climb, and he was far away from earshot, and it was useless to yell for help. Being a man of praise, and having been in the presence of God for an hour or more, he did the first thing that came to mind.

Jumping to his feet, he raised both hands toward heaven and shouted as loud as he could: "Praise the Lord!" The wild bull stopped dead in its tracks, turned around and fled in the other direction.[2]

This is similar to an incident in the Bible. King Abijah of Judah was surrounded by King Jeroboam's forces before and behind. 2 Chronicles 13:14-16:

>*They cried unto the LORD, and the priests sounded with the trumpets.*
>
>*Then the men of Judah gave a shout: and as the men of Judah shouted, it came to pass, that God smote Jeroboam . . .*
>
>*And the children of Israel fled before Judah: and God delivered them into their hand.*

Again, by their shout, God gave Joshua's army victory over Jericho.

>*So the people shouted when the priests blew with the trumpets: and it came to pass, when the people . . . shouted with a great shout, that the wall fell down flat, . . . and they took the city.*

God has given the weapon of praise as an instrument of authority over the devil. A few years ago, one of our sons had a roofing business here in San Antonio. He and his wife were away from the Lord at the time, and were not coming to church. One Saturday afternoon while they were visiting us, we pressed upon them their need to be in the House of God. Their response was definite: "It's summertime and very hot. Tomorrow morning we will be up on the roof early, completing our work before the afternoon heat." They said in no uncertain tones that there wasn't the slightest possibility of their coming to church.

The next morning on our way to Sunday School, my husband reached across the front seat of the car and said, "Honey, let's have an agreement prayer that our kids will be in church with us this morning." Driving down IH 10, I chuckled in almost unbelief at his suggestion. Had they not told us clearly that they were not giving God even a second thought? Yet, I put my hand into his, and as we drove along, we prayed an agreement prayer in faith, praising God that He would bring our kids to church that morning. As we continued praising God for this miracle, I peeked at my watch. It was exactly 9 a.m.

Later, when I came out of my Sunday School class and took my place at the organ, I noticed a couple on the back seat with sort of wild looking hair. They looked like they had dressed in a hurry and had been out in the wind. The service started and I needed to keep my mind on my music, *but who was that on the back seat?* I couldn't see them clearly, yet they looked too familiar for me to be mistaken. *It couldn't be them, they were out roofing*— and yet, the more I glanced away from the music to the back seat where my attention was drawn, I knew it was them.

After the service I rushed back to give them a big hug and asked her how it was that they got to come, and she answered: "We began roofing at 4 a.m. and had no intention of coming to church, but at straight up nine o'clock my husband jumped off the roof and said, 'Aw shucks honey, let's call it a day and go to church.'"

How did it happen? When we prayed and agreed together, then expressed our praises in the face of the impossible, we generated power in the heavenlies and activated God's promises. Today this son is serving the Lord—another answer to prayer and praise.

Psalm 149 shows the connection between praise and authority. In it praise takes on interesting dimensions. Verse one tells us to praise the Lord, sing unto the Lord a new song, and sing praises in the congregation of saints. Verse two challenges us to rejoice in our Creator, and to be joyful in our King (celebrate!). Verse three says to praise God in the dance (See also Luke 6:23), and to sing praises with the timbrel and harp. Verse five commands us to be joyful in glory, and to sing aloud upon our beds. All of this is given as a foundational background, preparing us for the last four verses. The final section tells us how to take authority over all evil.

Verse six says to have the high praises of God in our mouth, and a two edged sword in our hand. These two points are very exciting. High frequency sound waves are known to be a force that unites.

The instamatic camera is welded together with high frequency sound waves. High frequency sound waves are used to detect cracks in metal, and also to clean out dirty engines. Those who have experienced the power of high praises know that there is a cleansing that takes place through high praise, just as the high frequency sound waves cleanse, expose, and weld things together. Thus, high praises do these three things in the spiritual:

1. They cleanse our spirits

2. They detect and expose cracks in our metal

3. They weld us together in unity and God's bonding

The second part of verse six is also powerful. It speaks of *"the two edged sword."* That sword could be called "the two mouthed sword." God has spoken, and we speak. When we say what He said, that puts a two edged sword in our hand. This is a powerful tool for taking authority over demons when it is combined with praise. The mouth is called the rudder of the spirit.

Verses seven through nine reveal the purpose. It is to enable us to execute vengeance on demons (heathen), and punishment upon Satan's pawns (the unsaved). We are to bind their kings (their leading demons) with chains, and their nobles (trained demons) with fetters of iron. Praise is what gives us authority to perform this in the heavenlies.

Verse nine gives the final blow, and shows that this privilege is not limited to a selective few, it is an honor given to all of God's saints:

> *To execute upon them the judgment written: this honour have all his saints. Praise ye the LORD.*
>
> (Psalm 149:9)

We are to execute upon the demons the judgment written. Are we aware that the judgment written is that *"Death is swallowed up in victory"*(1 Corinthians 15:54)? Verse 26 says death is the last enemy to be destroyed. Jesus said in John 10:10:

> *The thief cometh not, but for to steal, and to kill, and to destroy: I am come that they might have life, and that they might have it more abundantly.*

70

Another favorite Scripture connecting praise with life is Psalm 102:18-20:

> *And the people which shall be created shall praise the LORD.*
>
> *For he hath looked down from the height of his sanctuary; . . . to loose those that are appointed to death.*

This says that people who actually have an appointment with death can be delivered by the weapon of praise and celebration. Praise enables us to take authority over circumstances and enter into celebrant faith to believe the promises of God.

A few years ago, before our son David was married, he blacked out on his way to college. A man informed us about it on our base C.B. radio. My husband immediately rushed to the address the man gave, and I went into our living room and began doing warfare in the Spirit.

I began to praise God for the gift of life for our son; that despite the fact that he had been frail from birth, and had had rheumatic fever, and though the doctors were wanting to do open heart surgery, I was going to praise my way above the dark clouds of doubt, fear, and death. There in our living room alone, exceedingly fearful in the natural, I began to celebrate Jesus and commanded in His name the cancellation of all assignments of the enemy.

While I was praising God, my husband and David arrived home. David was fine. Today he is our associate pastor, and the father of five beautiful sons. How faithful God is.

There are seven Hebrew words for praise given in Strong's Concordance[3]:

1. Towdah (#8426):   To extend the hands in thanksgiving. It is translated praise only a few times, but occurs many more times as thanksgiving. Psalm 50:23: *"Whoso offereth praise glorifieth me."*

2. Yadah (#3034):   To throw out the hands, enjoying God. Used over 90 times in the Old Testament. Psalm 134:2: *"Lift up your hands in the sanctuary, and bless the LORD."*

3. Hallal (#1984):   To celebrate and get vigorously excited. Used around 100 times in the Old Testament. Psalm 56:4: *"In God I will praise his word."*

4. Zamar (#2167):   To pluck the strings of an instrument and praise God with song, to orchestrate praise. Used exclusively in the Psalms, and occurs approximately 40 times. Psalm 149:3: *"Let them praise his name in the dance: let them sing praises unto him with the timbrel and harp."*

5. Barak (#1288):   To kneel, to bless, salute, praise God as the origin of power, success, prosperity and fertility. To hope, to quieten oneself before God, to be still. It is the only praise word denoting silence. Judges 5:2: *"Praise ye the LORD for the avenging of Israel."*

6. Tehillah (#8416): Singing in the Spirit or singing of Hallals. Used approximately 100 times. When we "tehillah" several good things happen:

   a. God inhabits our praise (Psalm 22:3).
   b. Creates reverence and awe (Exodus 15:11).
   c. Brings a desire for continual praise (Psalm 71:14).
   d. Power evangelism is released (Psalm 40:3): *"And he hath put a new song in my mouth, even praise unto our God: many shall see it, and fear, and shall trust in the LORD."*

7. Shabach (#7623): To shout, to triumph, to command, to glory - a noisy word. It is the exclamatory form of praise in a special sense and is found seven times in Scripture. (Psalm 22:3): *"But thou art holy, O thou that inhabitest the praises of Israel"* and (2 Chronicles 20:22): *"And when they began to sing and to praise, the LORD set ambushments against the children of Ammon, Moab, and Mount Seir, which were come against Judah; and they were smitten."*

These seven Hebrew words produce a progressive unfolding of the purposes of God for which we can take authority and change our circumstances through praise. When we celebrate in these seven different ways, it helps us see how big God is, and it shrinks the negatives and problems.

My favorite method of praise is to dance before the Lord. Especially when facing some problem, such as when we got that call on our C.B. radio about David. When I dance before the Lord, I remind the devil of his total defeat at Calvary, and that I am squashing his crushed head a little further into the dirt.

God told His people they would stomp on the necks of their enemies. This is what we do when we celebrate the Lord in exuberant praise. The only trace of Satan then is on the bottom of our shoes. He is defeated as we celebrate Jesus.

Paul Billheimer declares that though God is omnipresent, He is not everywhere in benign influence.[4] Wherever there is joyful, hilarious praise to Him, there God is dynamically and benevolently active. Psalm 22:3 says that God *"inhabitest the praises of Israel."* This means that where there is adoration, reverence, and acceptable praise, there God openly manifests His presence.

And God's presence always expels Satan. Satan is allergic to praise, so where there is massive, triumphant praise, Satan is paralyzed, bound, and banished. This enables us to take authority over evil with good. Romans 12:21 says: *"Be not overcome of evil, but overcome evil with good."*

The secret of overcoming faith is praise. James 4:7 says to resist the devil and he will flee. Since praise produces the divine presence of Jesus, it is a shield against satanic attack. Because praise is anathema to Satan, it is not only our defense, it is an offensive weapon. If you want to continually overcome, you must be a continuous praiser. David said in Psalm 34:1: *"I will bless the LORD at all times: his praise shall continually be in my mouth."*

He had a tremendous revelation of the power of praise. He set aside and dedicated an army of four thousand Levites whose sole occupation was to praise the Lord (1 Chronicles 23:5).

When Abraham passed his supreme test in Genesis 22 and willingly offered his only son Isaac as a Burnt Offering (a real sacrifice of praise), God said to him: *"Thy seed shall possess the gate of his enemies."* The promise was repeated to Abraham's daughter-in-law in Genesis 24:60:

Be thou the mother of thousands of millions, and let thy seed possess the gate of those which hate them.

Gates in the Bible speak of authority and access. In Matthew 16:18 Jesus said: *"I will build my church; and the gates of hell shall not prevail against it."* Again Jesus said in Luke 10:19:

Behold, I give unto you power to tread on serpents and scorpions, and over all the power of the enemy: and nothing shall by any means hurt you.

We have personally experienced the authority that praise brings. In our travels for ministry we have encountered severe storms both by ship and by plane. Once while we were on a large English ship returning from Japan, we were caught in a typhoon. They were unable to serve meals for forty eight hours. Water poured in and down the stairs like a river. The huge grand piano in the library sailed across the floor, and dishes flowed out of their cupboards and rattled down the halls breaking as they went. The most frightening part was when someone screamed: "Fire! Fire! The ship's on fire!" The billows of smoke poured down the halls. Waves the size of huge mountains banged against our cabin window like dark sea monsters.

The sky was black. There was nowhere to go. But as we prayed and praised God together, we knew He would bring us through. And He did. Though there was a lot of smoke, it was merely a small electrical fire, and was soon contained. The damage to the ship was several thousand dollars but no life was lost. After the storm passed over, the ocean was calm, the weather was beautiful, and we were safe.

I have never been fond of traveling. Even as a young girl, and a missionary's daughter, I experienced vicious storms and scary situations. My first few trips by plane were terrifying to me—engine trouble, wings packed with heavy ice, gas shortages, as well as severe thunder storms and wind.

Until around eight years ago, I avoided flying if at all possible. But when there came a time of special ministry in Japan, I knew God wanted me to overcome this fear. I asked Him for a Scripture. Immediately He gave me Luke 10:19; *"Nothing shall by any means hurt you."* Flying became a fascinating experience. With that Scripture in my heart, and praises on my lips, I actually enjoyed the flight to California. As we deplaned there, I found my spirit saying excitedly, "Where is that jumbo jet to Japan? Let's go for it."

I couldn't believe that was really me! And all the way to Japan, any time the seat belt sign came on, or there was a little turbulence, immediately that Scripture was there: *"Nothing shall by any means hurt you."* Praise overflowed my spirit. It was wonderful to be free from fear in this area, simply by taking authority in praise.

To be effective, praise must be massive, continuous, a full-time occupation, a fixed habit, and a way of life. To be able to take authority is to make a personal dedication to do this. I heard Judson Cornwall say: "You can praise by long distance, but worship is involvement." He also said, "Praise is what brings us into the presence of God, but worship is what we do after we get there."[5]

The Psalmist David said in Psalm 57:7: *"My heart is fixed, O God, my heart is fixed: I will sing and give praise."* Setting your will to praise instead of tensing up in a stressful situation gives you peace and authority when you could be getting upset. For years I've had the habit of praising God verbally when I'm in the car alone.

One morning as I arrived for a class I was teaching at International Bible College, a couple of students ran to my car and began to tell me a bunch of garbage that someone had said about me. None of it had any truth to it, and my first response was a feeling of indignation. Then I remembered my mighty tool of praise, and I determined not to let their foolish talk derail me from the inspiration bubbling in my spirit. I entered the classroom praising God for things just as they were, and I was not only free, I was all bubbly, and really ready to teach.

On another morning as I drove to the college praising God alone in the car, I was conscious that there was ice on the bridges and was driving slowly and carefully. Suddenly, a large white van crashed into my right side and we skidded around together for a little. Instead of tensing up, I continued praising God aloud, knowing that He had given dominion even over a dangerous situation. When our vehicles finally came to a stop, the young van driver apologized profusely, and promised to fix all the damages. Neither of us was hurt and we stood by the side of the road and prayed and thanked God together.

As we set our hearts to praise, we are enabled to rise above the circumstance and take authority over it. Anyone can do this at any time. It is a power-tool God has given us by which we walk in His authority, celebrating Him, and not the problem. Peter walked on the water when he focused on Jesus, but he began to sink when he looked at the waves. Praise diverts our attention from the problem to the bigness of God, and His ability and faithfulness to reign in every situation.

When we make a quality decision to praise Him regardless, we move into a position of authority. Praising God gives us authority over our emotions and our normal reactions by "fixing" our hearts. This comes through the quality decision to be a praiser at all times, which enables us to move into God-given authority. Praise celebrates Jesus—not the problem!

1. Billheimer, Paul E.; *Destined for the Throne* (Fort Washington, PA., Christian Literature Crusade, 1974), p.128.

2. Billheimer, p.127

3. Strong, James, S.T.D., LL.D.; *The Exhaustive Concordance of The Bible*, (Nashville: Abingdon Press, 1890), Hebrew and Chaldee Dictionary, seven Hebrew words for praise: #8426, #3034, #1984, #2167, #1288, #8416, #7623.

4. Billheimer, p.120.

5. Cornwall, Judson; pastor's retreat in California, teaching on worship.

9

Celebrate with the Agreement Prayer

Again I say unto you, That if two of you shall agree on earth as touching any thing that they shall ask, it shall be done for them of my Father which is in heaven.

(Matthew 18:19)

Prayer is an integral part of praise. It is the other wing of Isaiah's eagle which, along with praise, enables us to soar into God's heavenlies with fresh inspiration and renewed strength (Isaiah 40:31). Prayer balances praise just as one foot balances the other enabling us to walk without becoming weary and to run and not faint.

Ruth and I were several years into our marriage and ministry before we became acquainted with Matthew 18:19. In those days we were not aware of the impact of the agreement prayer. In looking back we can see how we were practicing it even before we knew its Scriptural basis.

I was born and raised in Cunningham, a small country town in the northeast corner of Texas. Though void of many things found in larger cities, one of the greatest assets of our community was an excellent school. We were taught high moral standards, and prayer and Bible reading were as much at home there as the ABCs.

Upon graduation from high school I was faced with a decision which I did not know how to handle. What were my life goals? What direction was I to take? My coach was eager to help me obtain a basketball scholarship at a nearby college. He graciously offered to guide me through the process. But just the year before, I had met the Lord in a summer revival, and was baptized with the Holy Spirit. There was a tug in my heart to go in another direction, but I was not sure.

One of my teachers was a Spirit filled Christian (she would later become my sister-in-law), and she took a special interest in me, suggesting that I consider going to Bible College. This brought me to a crossroad—would it be basketball or Bible College?

It was with Afton that I consciously entered into my first agreement prayer. As she was leaving for a week's trip she said, "Johnny, let's set this week aside for prayer about your future. I believe when I return we will both know the answer." I agreed to pray each day while she was gone. I knew very little about prayer at that time, but each day I made my way to a certain place in a wooded area and asked God to make His will clear to me.

Though my prayers were brief and there was no special revelation or anything sensational, by the end of the week the thought of college and basketball had drifted far away, and the desire for Bible College had become strong. Upon her return, Afton asked, "Did you receive an answer from the Lord?" "I believe I did. I believe it is God's will for me to go to Bible College," was my reply. She smiled, and we both knew that God had answered our agreement prayer.

It is said that "Eternity's doors swing on tiny hinges." What might appear to be a small decision could very well be a life-changing experience. So it was in my life. It was at Bible College that I fell in love with the Word of God and received my call to preach. It was there that I met Ruth Coote, who was to become my wife and my lifetime partner in ministry.

In 1954 I made my first trip to Japan, Ruth's birthplace. Her father, Leonard Coote, who had returned to Japan after World War II, invited me to come as the guest speaker for the New Year's Convention. The five weeks of every night ministry in churches, rented halls, and on the streets of Japan, completely revolutionized my life. I would never be the same again. The following year I was invited back and this time Ruth went with me.

During those two months in Japan, Ruth and I were overwhelmed with a burden for this country given to idolatry, with teeming millions of people who had not once heard a gospel message. While we were there we were praying in agreement together that God would show us what we could do for the masses who sat in darkness. As we were returning home on the plane, we compared notes and found that we had each received the same answer from the Lord—we must resign our church in San Antonio and return to Japan to help reap the harvest.

In the fall of 1956 we moved to Japan with our two sons. After our goods came through customs and we began to settle in to language study, we began to pray together that God would show us where our thrust of ministry should be. After several days of agreeing in prayer the direction for our ministry was revealed in a unique manner.

One morning, while kneeling in prayer, my eyes fell on my open Bible and a verse stood out as if it had been highlighted. It was Mark 1:38: *"Let us go into the next towns that I may preach there also; for therefore came I forth."*

I read it aloud to Ruth and we both agreed that this was to be the thrust of our ministry in Japan—going to the next towns, where Christ had not been preached. Immediately we ordered a tent and began the work of what is now known as THE NEXT TOWNS CRUSADE IN JAPAN.

As a result of our tent campaigns, small groups of believers began to form. It was exciting to see churches birthed in new towns. Several times God led us by degrees into progressive agreement prayers. It began with the vision of *The Next Towns Crusade* and the ordering of the tent. The day we made the order, we had no resources with which to pay for it. Yet, through the agreement prayer, God met the need, and on the day of its delivery, we were able to pay for it in full.

At our first crusade in the new tent, God gave us sixty-five beautiful young people, saved and excited about the Lord. But teenagers, though zealous and wonderful for the beginnings of a new church, don't have a financial base for buying land or a building.

When we had our second tent crusade, we asked God for adults as well as young people. To our amazement, this agreement prayer was also answered.

After each tent meeting, we began to have weekly services to establish the new believers. Now we were running out of nights, and how to care for these new Christians became a great concern. This stimulated another agreement prayer; that among our next converts God would bring in young men and women who would dedicate themselves to full time ministry. In a short time we had seven young men in the Ikoma Bible College, training as pastors: another answer to the agreement prayer.

After spending the better part of six years in missionary work in Japan, the Lord sent us back to the pastorate of Revival Temple in San Antonio. The ensuing years brought new understanding of God's Word for our day, and it was during this time that Matthew 18:19 became a rhema to us.

Time after time when facing difficult situations in ministry, in family relationships, or in various building programs, Ruth and I held hands together and prayed the agreement prayer. Over and over, God has supernaturally answered and given us tremendous miracles. The agreement prayer works, especially within the framework of praise and celebration.

In Matthew 18:15-20, Jesus taught about three important principles:

1. Confrontation for Offenses (verses 15-17).

2. Binding and Loosing (verse 18).

3. The Agreement Prayer (verses 19-20).

Jesus wanted us to know the power of the agreement prayer. Verses 15-17 show the importance of things being right between us and others, in order for the power of the agreement prayer to be fully released. The issue here is forgiveness when a brother wrongs us, and it is our responsibility to initiate reconciliation. The first step when there is an offense, is to go to the person alone (vs.15) and to gently confront the offense. If he listens, we have gained our brother. If he refuses, then we are to take one or two mature people with us, and to humbly make an appeal (vs.16).

If he refuses the second step, then Jesus said it is to be shared with the church leadership, that there may be intercessory and agreement prayer made for the situation. In wisdom then, one of the leaders can make an appeal. It is only after these steps have failed, and the offender refuses to listen to the church, that excommunication follows. Usually when done humbly, wisely, and according to the above steps, hearts melt together, and reconciliation follows. How wise the Lord is. If more Christians followed this pattern, there would be fewer splits and less heartaches.

Following this teaching on reconciliation, Jesus taught about binding and loosing in verse 18:

Verily I say unto you, Whatsoever ye shall bind on earth shall be bound in heaven: and whatsoever ye shall loose on earth shall be loosed in heaven.

This is a powerful promise. Most of us are not aware of the tremendous impact this can make, when we agree together to bind and loose. We can bind our loved ones to the heart and purpose of God, and loose them from evil spirits and any assignment Satan may have against them. We can bind them to the spirit of forgiveness and to God's joy and peace. Jesus wanted us to know this, and to use this power at our command.

The third step, that of the agreement prayer, is tied with the first two, and it is more effective when we are conscious of the power of all three.

Our prayers are definitely hindered when there is unforgiveness or negatives in our hearts or our speech. It is in this area that Satan often deceives people, trying to hinder through guilt and condemnation so that prayer becomes powerless. And if he can bring division between the very two who would otherwise be in agreement in prayer, he has weakened their effectiveness.

Many of us have heard Matthew 18:20 and used it as an excuse for the small crowd at church, as if it is saying that as long as you gather together in His name, the crowd (or lack of it) doesn't matter. But the true meaning is tied in with the agreement prayer of verse 19, for verse 20 begins with the word "for":

For where two or three are gathered together
in my name, there am I in the midst of them.

What this verse really means is that when two or three people are together in one accord and pray the agreement prayer, God will send His miracle answer. Combine this with praise and celebration, and you have power. But if there is division, anger, or misunderstanding, it is hard to get into a genuine agreement prayer. That's why confrontation for offenses, and binding and loosing are vitally important.

And as if to accentuate this even further, Jesus spent the entire rest of Matthew 18 teaching on forgiveness. It was in the next verse that Peter asked how many times he had to forgive his brother. Jesus answered: *"Seventy times seven."* Who among us has ever forgiven the same person 490 times?

In the following verses Jesus taught about the unmerciful servant who, though he himself had been forgiven much, he went out and found a servant who owed him only a fraction of what he himself had been forgiven, and without mercy, had him cast into prison. Verses 34 and 35 are a frightening warning on unforgiveness:

And his lord was wroth, and delivered him to the tormentors, till he should pay all that was due unto him.

So likewise shall my heavenly Father do also unto you, if ye from your hearts forgive not every one his brother their trespasses.

Forgiveness not only enables us to effectively pray the agreement prayer, it also prevents us from being delivered to the tormentors. How many people today are living in torment emotionally, mentally, and spiritually, because they have not forgiven? Forgiveness is not a feeling you must feel; neither is it dependent on whether or not the other apologizes. It is a quality decision you deliberately make. Right now, this moment, if a face is coming before your eyes in the spirit, say out loud, calling the person's name: "I forgive. I forgive!"

Total forgiveness gives you power in the agreement prayer. But the lack of it, will hinder your prayers and your faith.

One of the most effective teams for the agreement prayer is a husband and wife team. It is important that we walk together in one accord and forgiveness. Sometimes on their way to church, families quarrel over petty details. What is happening? Satan is doing his best to bring division and confusion, just at the moment when they really need to be in unity. He doesn't want them to celebrate in God's house or be involved in united prayer or miracles. He conquers by dividing.

These principles are vital to the church. When forgiveness flows, binding and loosing is powerful for the increase of harvest. It is wonderful when there is true unity and the people come together in the agreement prayer for miracles. Satan then trembles.

Since the agreement prayer has such power when used by a husband and wife team, it is important to avoid strife and division like the plague. You need each other to be in agreement against the powers of darkness, for your children, your church, and for the nation. Jesus said, *"If two of you shall agree . . ."*

The next time a problem arises, join hands and stand together on Matthew 18:19, and claim the promises of God. If you are single, find someone who will agree with you in prayer. And remember, Jesus said: *"Where two or three are gathered together in my name, there am I in the midst of them."* When we come together in agreement in His name, we have the promise of His presence and the assurance of His answer. So let's practice the agreement prayer within the framework of celebrating His promises.

10

Celebrate with the Sacrifice of Praise

The dictionary definition of sacrifice is to devote with loss: to offer to God, or to surrender in order to gain something. The word praise is defined as commendation; tribute or honor; gratitude; applause; to worship; to glorify. When the two words are formed together as they frequently are in Scripture, the meaning is full—to give honor and worship to God in full surrender, even when you don't feel like it.

Have you ever praised God when you felt like it was a sacrifice? This is not easy, but it brings with it tremendous victory when done deliberately.

Three verses formerly thought to be the ultimate in this area are in 1 Thessalonians 5:16-18:

> *Rejoice evermore.*
>
> *Pray without ceasing.*
>
> *In every thing give thanks: for this is the will of God in Christ Jesus concerning you* (author's emphasis).

There have been times when I didn't feel like rejoicing, praying, or giving thanks in anything. But it became easy when I focused on how great and wonderful God is. I could give thanks **in** everything, knowing that Jesus reigns. But then one day I read a stronger Scripture in Ephesians 5:20: *"Giving thanks always for all things unto God and the Father in the name of our Lord Jesus Christ"* (author's emphasis).

Give thanks *for* all things? That was hard to do. This verse was quickened to us when the marriage of one of our sons was breaking up. His wife had left him for another man, and almost every night he would call us, sobbing his heart out. And God expected us to thank Him *for* everything? This was hard to swallow. It was a terrible time for us. Our son was alone, hundreds of miles away in another state. Each night when he called, we could hear the anguish in his voice, and the hopelessness. We knew he was bordering on suicide, and all we could do was try to comfort him and cry out to God.

Were we to thank God for the pending divorce that would scatter his family? How we struggled with this. It was made even worse by our knowledge of how God abhors divorce. But God's Word is always true, even when it seems contradictory. So we began to thank God for the situation. It was hard to do.

As time went on, we became aware that our praising God for the divorce was actually a sacrifice of praise. We sure didn't feel like doing it, but did it daily in pure obedience to Him. As we continued to praise God daily for this difficult situation, it was amazing what began to happen.

Our son, who had been away from the Lord for several years, began to attend church again. He promised to God and to turn away from the life of sin he had known in the past. Something also happened in our hearts. As we praised God for things just as they were, we began to mellow toward our former daughter-in-law.

The anger and disappointment we had felt at first were replaced with forgiveness and compassion, both for her and the man she was living with. New faith birthed within us for the three children involved. The big miracle was that the court awarded the children to our son, in a state that nearly always gives them to the mother.

Paul and Silas obviously understood the power of the sacrifice of praise when they were in that dreadful, damp Philippian jail. They had just been beaten with many stripes (see Acts 16:23), and their hands and feet were held fast in stocks. Silas could easily have turned to Paul and accused him of misleading him. He could have asked, "Brother Paul, are you sure you heard from God that we should come to this area with the gospel?"

Instead, that night they sang their praises so loud, the prisoners heard them (see Acts 16:25). Would you feel like singing praises at a time like that? Their backs were bleeding and aching from the beating. The next day they faced possible execution. Instead of complaining, they sang and celebrated Jesus. That was the sacrifice of praise!

This kind of celebration releases the supernatural for us. Just as the miracle answer to our prayers came for our son during the time of his divorce, God's miraculous power was manifested for Paul and Silas at midnight.

God sent a great earthquake shaking the foundations of the prison and opening the doors. The jailor, thinking the prisoners had escaped, was ready to kill himself. But Paul stopped him, and right there, they had a prison revival, and the man and his whole house were saved. All the result of the sacrifice of praise.

Are you in a prison of depression or some other type of bondage? Begin offering to God the sacrifice of praise. Praise God for your situations just as they are, and watch miracles begin to happen. The sacrifice of praise releases the supernatural, and enables God to work mightily for you. It confuses Satan and makes him flee.

Psalm 42:3 describes David going through an emotional upheaval in his life, and he said: *"My tears have been my meat day and night, while they continually say unto me, Where is thy God?"* If you are going through something like that, turn to the Scripture and let God work out in you the same solution He did in David. In Psalm 42:5 David spoke to his own soul:

> *Why art thou cast down, O my soul? and why art thou disquieted in me? hope thou in God: for I shall yet praise him for the help of his countenance.*

The soul of man is the realm of the emotions, mind, and will, while man's spirit is the area of the conscience, intuition, and worship. David recognized that it was his soul that was upset, and in verse six he cried out to God: *"O my God, my soul is cast down within me: therefore will I remember thee."*

This is similar to the sacrifice of praise. At a time when we are in an emotional upheaval, the temptation is to sit down and have a good cry and enjoy a pity party. But instead, David deliberately decided to remember God, and he began to offer a sacrifice of praise despite his feelings that *"all thy waves and thy billows are gone over me"* (verse 7). Then David goes on to say: *"Yet the LORD will command his lovingkindness in the daytime, and in the night his song shall be with me."*

Three times in this section David asks his soul why it is cast down; the last verse in Psalm 42 and the last verse in Psalm 43 both begin with the same question: *"Why art thou cast down, O my soul?"* But each time it is asked, it is with a different emphasis. As he enters into the sacrifice of praise, determining to praise God regardless, the cause of his discouragement gets dimmer, and God's great power and faithfulness become more vivid.

The first time David asks the question of his soul, he follows it with *"I shall yet praise him for the help of his countenance"* (42:5). The second time, he follows it with *"I shall yet praise him, who is the health of my countenance, and my God"* (42:11).

Things are improving here, and it is obvious that the sacrifice of praise is doing its work in David. The third time he asks the question, (43:5) is after he has asked God to judge him and deliver him from an ungodly nation. He also makes a commitment to go to the altar of God in order to make God his exceeding joy, and to praise Him with his harp.

This third time when he asks the same question of his soul, it is almost as if to say, "There's nothing to be cast down about, since you can hope in God!" A different mood has taken over, though the words are the same. What has changed? He has been offering a sacrifice of praise which has enabled him to see beyond and above the negative.

No wonder David could say in Psalm 116:17 *"I will offer to thee the sacrifice of thanksgiving, and will call upon the name of the LORD."* Many years later, when the nation of Israel was about to be taken in the siege by Nebuchadnezzar, the prophet Jeremiah prophesied that though the nation would go into captivity and be scattered, the day would come when God would restore them and they would again be *"bringing sacrifices of praise, unto the house of the LORD"* (Jeremiah 17:26). In Jeremiah 33:10 and 11 he proclaimed an even stronger prophecy of restoration:

Thus saith the LORD; Again there shall be heard in this place, . . .

The voice of joy, and the voice of gladness, . . . the voice . . . of them that shall bring the sacrifice of praise into the house of the LORD. For I will cause to return the captivity of the land, as at the first, saith the LORD.

A clear command to the church is given in Hebrews 13:15:

By him therefore let us offer the sacrifice of praise to God continually, that is, the fruit of our lips giving thanks to his name.

The prophet Habakkuk was hurting deeply over the impending judgment on his nation because of their sins. He knew destruction was coming, and it disturbed him that God would use the wicked Chaldeans to punish the nation of Israel. And yet in the midst of this desolation He declared:

Although the fig tree shall not blossom, neither shall fruit be in the vines; the labour of the olive shall fail, and the fields shall yield no meat; the flock shall be cut off from the fold, and there shall be no herd in the stalls:

Yet I will rejoice in the LORD, I will joy in the God of my salvation.

The LORD God is my strength, and he will make my feet like hinds' feet, and he will make me to walk upon mine high places. To the chief singer on my stringed instruments.

(Habakkuk 3:17-19)

Habakkuk was singing his sacrifice of praise even in the face of total desolation, disruption and famine. Can you imagine a more bleak picture? But how it glorifies God when, regardless of circumstances or our feelings, He sees us look up to Him in perfect trust, celebrating His goodness, and hears us give to Him our true sacrifice of praise. This is true celebration.

11

Celebrate with Militant Praise

by David M. Bell

We are at war. War? Yes, war! The sides have polarized. The boundaries have been drawn. The battle has been set in array.

It's the forces of light against the powers of darkness. Jesus against Satan. The redeemed against the work of the wicked. Righteousness against iniquity. The prophetic anointing of God against the anointing of Satan. We, as the people of God, the bride of Christ, and soldiers of the Cross, are to be fighting the good fight of faith. This is the basis of our victory—our future—our destiny.

Do we really understand the essence of our destiny in Christ? It's easy to identify with the catch phrase "destined to win" and say "Yes, that is me. I'm destined to win."

But what actually is implied in this phrase is that we are destined to fight.

Winning is the result of a successful struggle or battle. There is no winning without a fight. There is no victory without warfare. Are we warriors? Are we militant? Are we violent in our outlook toward the enemy?

> *The kingdom of heaven suffereth violence, and the violent take it by force.*
>
> (Matthew 11:12)

God is not returning for an apathetic, passive, frail, sickly bride who does not care about the war, but a vibrant, healthy, militant, victorious bride that is immersed in the job of kicking in the gates of hell and taking our cities for God.

There is a new sound emerging across the land, as the people of God arise, hone their spiritual weaponry, and run to the battle. This sound is not just an ancillary, supplemental sound of accessory, but is a fundamental part of the battle itself. Where there is revival, there is this sound. Where there is victory, there is this sound. Where there is vitality in the church, there is this sound. Where there are motivated young people, there is this sound. Wherever there's something happening spiritually, you will hear this sound.

What is this sound? It is militant praise. Militant, high praises are resounding as God's people everywhere rise up in victory and begin to see the strongholds of the enemy fall. Militant means combative and aggressive. As we praise God, we are to do so in a combative and aggressive fashion, celebrating past victories, and anticipating future triumphs.

Let the high praises of God be in their mouth,
and a twoedged sword in their hand;

To execute vengeance upon the heathen, and
punishments upon the people;

To bind their kings with chains, and their
nobles with fetters of iron;

To execute upon them the judgment written:
this honour have all his saints.

(Psalm 149:6-9)

In this passage, the words *heathen* and *people* refer to the forces of Satan. The words *kings* and *nobles* refer to the leadership of Satan's forces. If we will allow the high, militant praises of God to be in our mouth, then we will not only see the enemy defeated but punished, and his field generals (kings and nobles) bound with chains and iron fetters.

A key phrase in the passage is *"in their mouth."* A closer examination of the original Hebrew renders it as *"be in their throat"* (as in swallowing something). This implies not only short bursts of praise, but a diet of praise. If we really want to see the enemy's forces and leadership bound with chains and fetters, then we must maintain a consistent diet of high praise and celebration.

Praise him with the sound of the trumpet:
praise him with the psaltery and harp.

Praise him with the timbrel and dance: praise
him with stringed instruments and organs.

(Psalm 149:3-4)

99

Sounds of Celebration

The words *timbrel* and *harp* speak clearly that God has ordained percussive (timbrel) and melodic (harp) instruments for use in voicing our praise to Him. For years, melodic (organs, piano and the like) instruments have been used in the church worship environment. However, in this day we are seeing a move toward a more percussive (dynamic) sound, as the church is awakening to the war, to the victory, and the celebrant lifestyle.

Every manner of instrument is now being used in praise of our King: pianos, organs, brass, woodwinds, electronic keyboards, music computers, guitars, drums and percussion, all for the purpose of magnifying our Lord and celebrating our victory in Him. God is raising up a praising generation who are the most exciting, dynamic, power-filled people in the world—a people of destiny.

> *And the LORD shall cause his glorious voice to be heard, and shall show the lighting down of his arm, with the indignation of his anger, and with the flame of a devouring fire, with scattering, and tempest, and hailstones.*
>
> *For through the voice of the LORD shall the Assyrian be beaten down, which smote with a rod.*
>
> *And in every place where the grounded staff shall pass, which the LORD shall lay upon him, it shall be with tabrets and harps: and in battles of shaking will he fight with it.*
>
> (Isaiah 30:30-32)

Just as it is described in verse 30, God's voice is being heard today, and the work of the evil one is being destroyed by His hand. How does the enemy hear God's voice?

Through the unified, celebrant, prophetic, militant praises of His redeemed. That means you! That means me. Are you praising Him? Celebrating Him? Prophetically? With a celebrant spirit? Demonstratively? Militantly?

In verse 31 of Isaiah 30, we see that through the voice of the Lord shall our enemy (the Assyrian) be beaten down. This is the unified voice of our praise to the King. In verse 32 we find that every place where the grounded staff (the rod of God's deliverance) shall pass, it shall be accompanied by prophetic, militant praise music, with both a melodic (harps) and percussive (tabrets) emphasis. For those aspiring to play a musical instrument in worship services, this is a most important passage.

It is critical that today's musician command not only technical expertise in his instrument, but also the ability to flow in the prophetic realm, providing an atmosphere which will foster a revelation of Jesus, His power, and His deliverance. We sing and play prophetic, militant praise music, offering it to the Lord. He, then uses it in warfare " . . . *in battles of shaking will he fight with it*" (verse 32).

This truth is also demonstrated by Jehoshaphat's praise band in 2 Chronicles 20. The nation of Judah was under attack from the nations of Ammon, Moab, and the inhabitants of Mount Seir. Verse 17 gives the prophetic utterance of one of the Levites of Judah:

> *Ye shall not need to fight in this battle: set yourselves, stand ye still, and see the salvation of the LORD with you.*

What did Judah do? King Jehoshaphat appointed a praise band (see verse 21), to praise the beauty of His holiness, and to proclaim His mercy. Verse 22 reads:

*And when they began to sing and to praise,
the LORD set ambushments against the children
of Ammon, Moab, and mount Seir, which were
come against Judah; and they were smitten.*

Furthermore, it states in verse 23 that these enemies
actually destroyed one another. Our exaltation of Jesus
brings the enemy into a state of confusion, so that the
kingdom of Satan actually begins to war within itself. This
passage again bears out the truth that when we offer high,
celebrant praise to our God, the enemy is punished, just
as he was in Psalm 149:6,7.

Other passages of Scripture demonstrate this truth,
such as the story of the victory over Jericho in Joshua
6:20,21; Gideon's triumph in Judges 7:20-22; and Paul &
Silas' deliverance in Acts 16:25,26. In each case, the
mighty rod of God's deliverance was manifested through
the militant, celebrant praises of His people.

God is awakening His church and fashioning a
glorious, victorious army which will do great exploits in
this final hour. In Joel 3: 9-10 we read:

*Prepare war, wake up the mighty men, let all
the men of war draw near; let them come up:*

*Beat your plowshares into swords, and your
pruninghooks into spears: let the weak say, I am
strong.*

It's time we answer this call, arise to a new excellence
in our praise, a new aggressiveness in our celebration,
and a new urgency in our militant expression. Jesus is our
champion. Through Him we shall do valiantly. He it is

Who defeats every enemy. He is worthy of highest Praise.
Crown Him! Laud Him! Give Him all honor, and win!

12

Celebrate with Triumphant Praise

Many books have been written in recent years on *spiritual warfare*. Some have seemed almost contradictory, as the challenge comes from one direction telling us we must fight, while from another direction the emphasis is that we need not do anything, because Jesus did it all. Where is the balance?

Scripture is rich with the challenge that we are to be winners. God said through Jeremiah 1:10:

See, I have this day set thee over the nations and over the kingdoms, to root out, and to pull down, and to destroy, and to throw down, to build, and to plant.

But how? God's Word is always the basis. As if in answer to our question "how?" God said in verse 12, for *"I will hasten my word to perform it."* Another key is given in Jeremiah 15:20:

> *And I will make thee unto this people a fenced brazen wall: and they shall fight against thee, but they shall not prevail against thee: for I am with thee to save thee and to deliver thee, saith the LORD.*

Three times in Ephesians 6, we are told to stand. Ephesians 6 is known as the Army Chapter. It is here that we are given the list of our pieces of armor for the battle. In verses 11, 13, and 14 we are told repeatedly to stand:

> *Put on the whole armour of God, that ye may be able to **stand** against the wiles of the devil. . . .*
>
> *Wherefore take unto you the whole armour of God, that ye may be able to withstand in the evil day, and having done all, to **stand.***
>
> ***Stand** therefore, having your loins girt about with truth, and having on the breastplate of righteousness* (author's emphasis).

This section on spiritual warfare in Ephesians 6 begins with verse 10: *"Finally, my brethren, be strong in the Lord, and in the power of his might."*

Two issues stand out here: (1) be strong, and (2) stand.

How do we do this? Especially when we are under demonic attack, sick in body, discouraged, oppressed, facing impossible situations?

(1) Praise. Nehemiah 8:10 says, *"The joy of the LORD is your strength."* So, to be strong for the war, and to triumph, praise is our priority.

(2) Stand. How do we do this, when everything about us seems to be crashing at our feet? When finances are bad, when people are criticizing and we are misunderstood? Stand. But how?

It is here that the Scriptures become unchanging, solid, secure, sure. How do we stand? Get a word from the Word, a promise from God, and then declare it in your times of prayer and praise. Remind God of His Word. Say it verbally. Tell Him you are standing on His promise. Tell Satan hands off, in the mighty name of Jesus, because you are standing on God's Word, and will not (by God's grace), back down. Proverbs 12:7 says: *"The wicked are overthrown, and are not: but the house of the righteous shall stand."*

Isaiah declared *"The grass withereth, the flower fadeth: but the word of our God shall stand for ever"* (Isaiah 40:8).

It came as a shock to me a few years ago that God has given us the authority to command Him. Recently I was teaching on this and a lady challenged me until I was able to direct her to the Scripture in Isaiah 45:11:

Thus saith the LORD, the Holy One of Israel, and his Maker, Ask me of things to come concerning my sons, and concerning the work of my hands command ye me.

The triumph of praise then, is when we face an enemy, we must praise and celebrate God regardless of situations, standing firm on His promises. This is spiritual warfare.

This is standing back and letting God do it. Nehemiah 4:20 says: *"Our God shall fight for us."*

How then do we fight in this war? Certainly not by beating the air. Paul said in 1 Corinthians 9:26: *"I therefore so run, not as uncertainly; so fight I, not as one that beateth the air."*

When we worry, get upset, lose our temper, have a pity party, or question God, we are just beating the air. That's not fighting, for it is not standing. Yes, Jesus has gone before, He has fought and won the war, He has done it all, but for us to be able to take the spoils, we must stand.

This is the praise-life that triumphs. It is founded upon the promises of God. It is praise that hooks into a promise and won't let go. When things continue to go in reverse, it still declares what God has declared, and will not be denied. Abraham stood firmly on the promised word even when circumstances dictated defeat. He believed that God *"calleth those things which be not as though they were"* (Romans 4:17).

James 4:7 says, *"Resist the devil, and he will flee from you."* We do this by standing firmly on God's Word, and praising Him. Satan hates the anointed praise of Jesus. There are nine specific reasons for Satan's intolerance to praise and why he flees when he hears it:

1. **Confusion** - When a Christian praises God in the midst of negatives, Satan is confused, and in his confusion pits himself against his demons, dividing his authority. He sees no reason for the Christian to be praising.

2. **Resurrection Remembered** - Praise reminds Satan of Christ's resurrection. It reminds him that Whom he thought he had slain forever, arose, took the keys to death, hell, and the grave, and provided salvation for us all. This is Satan's ultimate defeat, and he doesn't want to hear about it.

3. **Church Built Up** - Because praising Jesus builds up Zion. Satan is not welcome, cannot dwell there. It is a holy hill, and holiness and iniquity cannot coexist. Where true worship is, sin is exposed, dealt with, and the worker of iniquity cast out. Judgment begins at the house of the Lord. We must understand the awesomeness of this when we praise. It is important to maintain a clean vessel so that we may be ready for the Master's use.

4. **The Truth** - Because praise of Jesus is truth, and the father of lies does not want to hear truth, he leaves. In lifting the name of Jesus in praise, we proclaim truth: Jesus is awesome. Wonderful! Majestic! Powerful! Satan knows this is true, but can't stand to hear it. Jesus made Satan flee by quoting Scripture (truth). That is why Scripture choruses are powerful in worship. Satan flees.

5. **Births the Prophetic** - Because praise gives birth to the prophetic anointing causing the gifts of the Spirit to flow forth, this brings deliverance to the captives which Satan has

bound. Satan hates to be around when Jesus reveals Himself through His people.

6. **Binds Evil Forces** - Praise binds Satan's kings and nobles (his leadership), and renders them powerless. Psalm 149:7-9 shows that God has given us the honor of executing His judgment through our militant, high praises.

7. **The Future** - Praise reminds Satan of his future. He is doomed to burn eternally in the lake of fire. Though he may have won a few skirmishes, when we praise and celebrate Jesus our King, we punish Satan, and he is reminded of his ultimate destination.

8. **Most Highly Anointed** - Satan can't tolerate music more highly anointed than his. Hebrews 1:9 says that those who hate iniquity and love righteousness have a higher anointing. Lucifer was anointed to be the lead musician in heaven (Ezekiel 28:14), but he fell, due to self worship. Musicians are easily intimidated by other musicians. Can you imagine how Satan feels when he hears anointed music which he cannot begin to comprehend, and certainly cannot duplicate? We have records of him fleeing in Scripture (as when David played his harp before Saul).

9. **God's Soldiers** - Satan knows that where anointed praise is ascending, there are

anointed vessels (soldiers of the cross) nearby, ready to storm the gates of hell to cut asunder Satan's chains of darkness. Satan's only weaponry is his bluffing lies and false accusations. But when God's people praise the name of Jesus, it neutralizes lies and accusations, and brings us back to the power of the cross where sin is cancelled once and for all. Jesus said in Matthew 16:18: *"Upon this rock I will build my church; and the gates of hell shall not prevail against it."*

Jesus said the gates of hell shall not prevail against the church. Through praise and worship, Christians release the power to open the gates of hell and prevail over them, setting free those who are in the agony of Satan's bondage, be it drugs, disease, poverty, lust, whatever.

Here are some phrases and principles in Scripture, which demonstrate the power of dynamic praise:

1. The battle is the Lord's. (1 Samuel 17:47)

2. Shout for the battle. (1 Samuel 17:20)

3. Be a fortress for God's people. (Jeremiah 6:27)

4. Run to the war. (Revelation 9:9)

5. Don't beat the air. (1 Corinthians 9:26)

6. We war not after the flesh. (2 Corinthians 10:3)

7. War a good warfare. (1 Timothy 1:18)

8. The battle is not to the strong nor the race to the swift. (Ecclesiastes 9:11)

9. Wherever your feet shall tread shall be yours. (Deuteronomy 12:24)

10. No one shall be able to stand before you. (Joshua 1:5)

11. Having done all, stand! (Ephesians 6:13)

12. He teacheth my hands to war. (Psalm 18:34)

13. Teach the next generation, war. (Judges 3:2)

14. Our God shall fight for us. (Nehemiah 4:20)

15. There is no discharge in this war. (Ecclesiastes 8:8)

16. Be strong for the battle. (2 Chronicles 25:8)

17. The Lord is able to give thee much more. (2 Chronicles 25:9)

Thus with the sounds of celebration and war, let us make triumphant praise our lifestyle in all situations.

13

Celebrate a Lifestyle of Praise

by J. Nathan Bell

"Why was I born?" the adolescent asks. And the question becomes more complex as the years roll by. The young college student seeks desperately to find the purpose for which he exists. The middle aged and elderly often look back and wish they had set different goals, or had lived their lives differently, feeling their goals have never been fulfilled.

Each person at the time of his birth has an attainable purpose. This purpose cannot be measured or eclipsed by someone else's achievement.

Many excellent explanations have been given as to why God created man. I've heard dynamic messages on God's love, and His reasons for choosing man though weak, inconsistent, and fickle, as the top priority of His creation. But each interpretation comes back to one big reason: God desires man's voluntary fellowship.

If God created us for communion how does this line up with our chosen vocation in life? How does it ultimately create a sense of fulfillment as to our life purpose? When the purpose is to have close fellowship with God, the fulfillment develops through a lifestyle of praise.

Praise brings dynamic results whether it is directed toward God or to our fellow man. Praise carries with it a desire to reciprocate. Have you ever found yourself praising one of your peers and at the same time feeling that you would refuse him should he ask you to do something for him? Of course not, you would desire to bless him.

Sincere praise brings with it a willingness to accommodate. Coincidentally, the person we are praising is also more inclined to accommodate our wishes. How much more, when we have a lifestyle of praising God, we find it easy to obey and with joy seek first His kingdom.

The praising lifestyle takes us a step beyond the salvation experience. The purpose of God in creating us is satisfied when we progress into the dimension of fellowship with Him through praise and celebration.

In Psalm 18:49 King David said, *"Therefore will I give thanks unto thee, O LORD, among the heathen, and sing praises unto thy name."*

Obviously David offered praise to God at times other than when he attended the place of worship. Even in the midst of the heathen he gave praise unto God. I can imagine him entering a boardroom of heathen businessmen, raising his hands and celebrating the Lord.

David introduces us to a real lifestyle of praise. He said in Psalm 34:1, *"I will bless the LORD at all times: his praise shall continually be in my mouth."*

Again in Psalm 35:28, *"And my tongue shall speak of thy righteousness and of thy praise all the day long."*

Some may question using David as an example, since he was king, and was doubtless allowed idiosyncrasies. Idiosyncrasies? Hardly. Praise is the lifestyle that God loves. It is a return to His original plan for mankind. And if this lifestyle of praise earned David the reputation of being a man after God's own heart, how can we miss by following his example? Whether it be in the workplace, at home, or in the grocery store, God's blessings abound on those who praise Him.

If the conversation at work is not conducive to Christianity, how can we openly praise God? Take the initiative, change the subject. The three Hebrew children are a striking example of this.

Shadrach, Meshach, and Abednego were taken from their family to Babylon. They were forced into a lifestyle that was foreign to them. The food was different. The society was different. The religion was different. Their whole life was turned upside-down, except for their lifestyle of praise, which they brought with them into their captivity.

Though the Bible doesn't give details about their praises, their stand for God erases any doubt that praising was their lifestyle. As the conversation in Babylon centered on the great idol that all must worship, the three Hebrews continued to speak praises only to God. Called before the king and asked why they would not bow down, their answer was definite—they would only praise their great Jehovah. And walking in the midst of the fiery furnace, accompanied by a fourth man, described by the king as "The Son of God," they surely were praising God. This is the praising lifestyle.

I recall a Superbowl game during the heyday of the Pittsburgh Steelers. Seconds were left in the game and the Steelers were behind a few points, with the entire season on the line. All of a sudden the football came loose and was bouncing from one player to another.

Suddenly out of nowhere came Franco Harris. Stumbling as he reached for the ball, he clasped it in his arms and blindly stumbled into the end zone for the winning touchdown. It was an astonishing play and for a few seconds no one was sure if it was a legal, countable touchdown. But it went into the books as the winner.

The following day everyone on the job was singing the praises of Franco Harris. It didn't matter that he probably didn't even know he had the ball until the play was over. It was impressive how all that day everyone wanted to sing Franco's praises.

How much more, when we focus on God? There are unlimited reasons for us to praise Him. He is our creator. Jesus, our Savior, took the keys of death, hell, and the grave from the archenemy Satan. We all without exception have innumerable things for which to praise God. If we would look for them, there are many ways to make every topic that comes up an item of praise.

What about the person who is not eloquent? How can he enter into this praising lifestyle? When our youngest son was three, I had trouble understanding his speech. But when he crawled up into my lap and looked up into my face with those trusting eyes, saying in his own way "I love you," it didn't matter that he wasn't eloquent. It wouldn't have mattered if the whole world had heard him stutter. What meant everything to me was my son was giving me praise.

Our lifestyle of praise does not have to be eloquent. Matthew 21:16 says, *"Out of the mouth of babes and sucklings thou hast perfected praise."*

Babies show praise to their parents with goos and gahs, smiles and laughter. This brings such joy to the hearts of the parents! How much more does our Father in heaven rejoice when we step beyond just the salvation experience, into the praising lifestyle which was the purpose for our birth?

Not only does the praising lifestyle honor God's purpose for our lives, but it moves us into another dimension. It brings us into an automatic seeking of God's kingdom first, bringing our vocation into proper balance with our skills.

Praise Him for having a name above all others. Praise Him for His will and kingdom being established from eternity. Praise Him for His provision, for keeping us from evil. Psalm 115:17 says, *"The dead praise not the LORD."* Does this indicate that those who praise not, are dead? Psalm 150:6 says, *"Let every thing that hath breath praise the LORD."*

Let's be alive and establish a lifestyle of praise by celebrating Jesus daily.

14

Celebrate with Wholehearted Praise

There's an interesting Hebrew word used in Scripture, which means undivided, complete, perfect, and wholehearted. The word in the Hebrew is *shalem*. In 1 Kings 8:61, Solomon challenged his people with it:

> *Let your heart therefore be perfect* [shalem] *with the LORD our God, to walk in his statutes, and to keep his commandments, as at this day* (author's insertion).

King David, in his fatherly blessing to his young son, Solomon, used the same word *shalem* in 1 Chronicles 28:9:

Know thou the God of thy father, and serve him with a perfect [shalem] *heart and with a willing mind: for the LORD searcheth all hearts, and understandeth all the imaginations of the thoughts: if thou seek him, he will be found of thee; but if thou forsake him, he will cast thee off for ever* (author's insertion).

David also used this word *shalem* in his prayer for Solomon in 1 Chronicles 29:19, *"Give unto Solomon my son a perfect* [shalem] *heart"* (author's insertion).

One of my favorite Scriptures is found in 2 Chronicles 16:9, where God speaks about the *shalem* heart:

For the eyes of the LORD run to and fro throughout the whole earth, to show himself strong in the behalf of them whose heart is perfect [shalem] *toward him* (author's insertion).

If there is anything God abhors, it is division. This is not only division in the sense of disunity in a church, or a home, but He also abhors division of the heart. In Revelation 3:16 He tells us He so abhors a divided heart, He wants to spew us out when we are lukewarm:

So then because thou art lukewarm, and neither cold nor hot, I will spue thee out of my mouth.

But how God loves the *shalem* heart. (Wholehearted, undivided, perfect, complete!) As a little girl, I remember how puzzled I was about Genesis 17:1, where God commanded Abraham to walk before Him and *"be perfect.*" I remember thinking, "That's impossible. No one can be perfect." It seemed like an outrageous command.

I ran with my Bible to Mother and said, "This can't be right. No one can be perfect. God is demanding too much." My mother always had the perfect answer for Scriptures that puzzled us. She would say, "God is much bigger than we are, and though we don't understand today, someday He will make it plain."

When I learned the meaning of the Hebrew word *shalem*, I realized that what God was saying to Abraham was, not that he should be perfect in the sense that we judge perfection, but that he should be wholehearted toward his God.

This was confirmed again in the account of Noah and the flood. One year, as we began reading the Bible through on New Year's day, when I came to Genesis 6:9, I was stunned by what God said about Noah:

> *These are the generations of Noah: Noah was a just man and perfect in his generations, and Noah walked with God.*

No wonder God could trust Noah to not only build the ark, but to also begin a whole new society after the flood. God saw in Noah three valuable traits:

1. He was just.

2. He had a *shalem* heart (perfect—wholehearted).

3. He walked with God.

What a tremendous person Noah must have been. These three traits challenged me. To be just, to be wholehearted, and to walk with God. Noah helped me to begin to see what God really meant. What God wants is a *shalem* heart (wholehearted toward Him), in everything we do, and especially in our praises.

This exploded in my heart—how that God wants us to "do with our might what our hands find to do" (see Ecclesiastes 9:10). All of us love enthusiasm and vibrancy. The word enthusiasm comes from the root "enthusio" which means filled with God. How much more should our praises be with all our heart.

Two of my sisters live in the Dallas area, and anytime we go to their homes for a visit, we can count on them running out to the car with big, excited smiles and hugs. This is a most wonderful, warm welcome. Our sisters' excited welcome is like a celebration of our arrival—filled with enthusiasm! It is the same response God wants from us: wholehearted, *shalem,* adoration, praise, and worship.

Did you ever shake hands with someone, and feel that they gave you a "dead fish handshake?" I wonder sometimes if God doesn't feel that way about us, when we fail to bring to Him a *shalem* wholehearted attitude of love and adoration.

Wholehearted praise is not without its critics. The flesh would rather cater to pride and center on the appearance of things. David danced with joy when the ark was coming home. But not Michal—she did not participate in the celebration and scorned his wholehearted worship. As a result, she was barren to the day of her death. (See 2 Chronicles 15:29).

Undaunted by her scorn, David declared with a *shalem* heart in 2 Samuel 6:22:

*And I will yet be more vile than thus, and will
be base in mine own sight: and of the maidservants
which thou hast spoken of, of them shall I be had
in honour.*

Barrenness and half-heartedness are closely related.
To be fruitful in this tremendous day of God's last harvest,
we must ask God for a *shalem* heart. We must set our will
even now, to strip away all excuses, all pride, and anything
that would keep us from being wholehearted for God.

William Booth Clibborn wrote a little booklet entitled
Too Much that was a great blessing to me as a teenager.
On its cover, there was a picture of a chalice of wine that
was spilling over onto everything. That picture has stayed
with me for years. God wants us to live in the overflow!

This comes as we pour out our love to Him with all of
our hearts. Two of my favorite Scriptures relate to this:

*Therefore, my beloved brethren, be ye stedfast,
unmoveable, **always abounding** in the work of the
Lord, forasmuch as ye know that your labour is
not in vain in the Lord.*

(1 Corinthians 15:58, author's emphasis)

There are three valuable traits we must go after if we
are to live in God's constant overflow:

1. Be steadfast (Consistent, faithful, loyal).

2. Be unmovable (No compromise, stand firm).

3. Be a servant (Abound in every area).

This can only come as we have a *shalem* heart toward God, a heart that is constantly celebrating Jesus.

My other favorite Scripture is:

> *God is able to make all grace abound toward you; that ye, always having all sufficiency in all things, may **abound** to every good work.*
> (2 Corinthians 9:8, author's emphasis)

The account of King Solomon is one of the saddest in history. Solomon, the wisest man who ever lived, because of his divided heart, became the world's greatest fool. The good years of his reign are called the "Golden Years" of Israel. Those were the years his heart was wholly given to God. At the dedication of the Temple he made a huge scaffold upon which he publicly kneeled down before the Lord, and lifting his hands toward heaven, called on God's help for his kingdom. Then he offered 22,000 oxen and 120,000 sheep. His worship, his praise, and his gifts were lavish and wholehearted. Even his prayer that day, as he knelt humbly before his people was a heart-cry of wholehearted worship:

> *O LORD God of Israel, there is no God like thee in the heaven, nor in the earth; which keepest covenant, and showest mercy unto thy servants, that walk before thee with all their hearts.*
> (2 Chronicles 6:14)

This wholehearted, exciting worship was also caught by the singers and musicians, creating such glory, the priests could not stand to minister. Can you imagine them all on their faces on the floor? The celebration was tremendous: 120 trumpeters and singers became one voice:

> *As the trumpeters and singers were as one,*
> *. . . when they lifted up their voice with the*
> *trumpets and cymbals and instruments of music,*
> *and praised the LORD, . . . that then the house*
> *was filled with a cloud, even the house of the*
> *LORD.*
>
> (2 Chronicles 5:13)

Solomon's fame spread around the world, and famous people came to see for themselves this wise king with the *shalem* heart. The Queen of Sheba left saying, *"The half was not told me"* (1 Kings 10:7). Peace, wisdom, riches and prosperity were the norm during these wonderful golden years of Solomon's early reign.

The tragedy began in 1 Kings 11:1 where it states that Solomon loved many strange women who turned away his heart (verse 3). Verse four of this chapter is one of the saddest parts of this glorious history of Israel's golden years:

> *When Solomon was old, that his wives turned*
> *away his heart after other gods: and his heart was*
> *not perfect with the LORD his God, as was the*
> *heart of David his father.*

And because his heart was no longer perfect toward the Lord, and had turned after other gods, God had to rend the kingdom away from his son. The wisest man, became the world's greatest fool.

As a little girl, I was sometimes puzzled as to why God called David *"a man after his own heart"* (1 Samuel 13:14) when his sins were so conspicuous. But it was David's *shalem* heart that made him delightful to God.

125

Over and over in the Psalms David spoke of praising God with his whole heart. In Psalm 9:1, David says, *"I will praise thee, O LORD, with my whole heart; I will show forth all thy marvellous works."* And again in Psalm 111:1, *"I will praise the LORD with my whole heart, in the assembly of the upright, and in the congregation."* And in Psalm 138:1, *"I will praise thee with my whole heart: before the gods will I sing praise unto thee."*

No wonder God loved David. He was enthusiastic about God, so God was enthusiastic about him. Someone once said: "If you make God's business your business, then God will make your business His business." If we celebrate the Lord, He will also celebrate us.

The Christian walk is exciting, joyous, and wonderful, when we have an undivided, *shalem* heart toward God. If you have had a half-hearted attitude toward the church, or toward the Bible, or toward the Lord Himself, make a decision now that you are going to be wholehearted about the things that really count, and let God birth in you a true *shalem* heart. This can begin in you a constant spirit of celebration.

Another favorite Scripture of mine is Ecclesiastes 9:10:

> *Whatsoever thy hand findeth to do, do it with thy might; for there is no work, nor device, nor knowledge, nor wisdom, in the grave, whither thou goest.*

Here the wise man was reminding us of the importance of being wholehearted in everything we do, be it a great challenge, or a tiny task. At best, our life is short, and we have only one opportunity to live life at its best. And that "best" that God wants us to have, results from a *shalem* heart. When Jesus is lord, and our lives are a wholehearted praise to Him, we then fulfill the true purpose for which we were born. A celebrating, wholehearted praiser with a *shalem* heart produces a wonderful lifestyle of constant, enthusiastic overflow!

15

This Celebrating Generation

The Bible speaks of a specific time when God will have mercy on Zion, even a set time when He will favor her, in Psalm 102:12-18:

> *But thou, O LORD, shalt endure for ever; and thy remembrance unto all generations.*
>
> *Thou shalt arise, and have mercy upon Zion: for the time to favour her, yea, the set time, is come.*
>
> *For thy servants take pleasure in her stones, and favour the dust thereof.*
>
> *So the heathen shall fear the name of the LORD, and all the kings of the earth thy glory.*

When the LORD shall build up Zion, he shall appear in his glory.

He will regard the prayer of the destitute, and not despise their prayer.

This shall be written for the generation to come: and the people which shall be created shall praise the LORD.

Obviously the writer knew that these words were written for a future generation of God's people. The Psalmist foresaw a generation of praisers, a people "created" or brought together at the time when He restores His church and builds her up in preparation for His soon coming.

We believe this is speaking of our generation, a time when God's people everywhere are entering into new dimensions of praise and celebration; thus, we speak of our generation as a "Praising Generation."

"Zion" in this passage refers to the church. Verses 19 through 21 make this very clear:

For he hath looked down from the height of his sanctuary; from heaven did the LORD behold the earth;

To hear the groaning of the prisoner; to loose those that are appointed to death;

To declare the name of the LORD in Zion, and his praise in Jerusalem;

It was in natural Zion, the city of Jerusalem, that spiritual Zion, the church, was born. On the Day of Pentecost the glory from the heavenly sanctuary came forcefully into the waiting earthly temples. Spiritual Zion was established and from the one hundred twenty disciples on the Day of Pentecost it has grown into a mighty force in the earth. Now the Lord is favoring His church with restoration revival and preparing her for that day when He shall present to Himself *"a glorious church."*

The word Zion means fortress. The first mention of Zion is in 2 Samuel 5:7. The Jebusites had fortified themselves in one of the hills of Jerusalem to resist and defy King David. But David prevailed and *"took the stronghold of Zion; the same is the city of David."*

Zion and the city of David became synonymous terms, and referred to a particular area of Jerusalem given over to the reigning of King David and the worship of Jehovah. It was on the hill of Zion and in the City of David that the tent was pitched for the ark of the covenant when David brought it up with joy from the house of Obededom. The presence of the ark made Zion the spiritual center of the kingdom.

1 Chronicles 15 and 16 tell of David bringing back the ark and establishing worship around the clock at the door of the tent under which it was placed. These chapters contain principles which are a pattern for worship today:

1. **Preparing a Place for the Presence of the Lord** - *"David, . . . prepared a place for the ark of God, and pitched for it a tent"* (15:1). It is possible to be so busy in our activities that we fail to give proper place for the presence of the Lord, and for praise and worship in our services.

2. **Gathering the People Together in Unity** - *"David gathered all Israel together to*

*Jerusalem, to bring up the ark of the LORD
unto his place, which he had prepared for
it* (15:3). God qualifies His leaders to
gather His people together in unity. Psalm
133 tells us that where God's people are
together in unity, *"there the LORD
comanded the blessing, even life
forevermore."* We should guard unity with
our life.

3. **Sanctification** - [David] *said unto them, Ye
are the chief of the fathers of the Levites:
sanctify yourselves, both ye and your
brethren, that ye may bring up the ark of
the LORD God of Israel unto the place that
I have prepared for it* (15:12). No matter
how evil our environment, God is still a
holy God, and demands separation from
sin. He will not tolerate sin in the lives of
His people, especially those who would be
worshipers and leaders.

4. **Seeking Him After the Due Order** - *"The
LORD our God made a breach upon us,
for that we sought him not after the due
order. So the priests and the Levites
sanctified themselves to bring up the ark
of the LORD God of Israel* (15:13,14). The
first effort to bring back the Ark resulted
in chaos. They used the method of the
Philistines and had the ark on a new cart
pulled by oxen. The oxen stumbled, (they
always will, when we use the world's
methods), Uzza reached out to steady it,

and was struck dead. Death results when we neglect God's principles. The second time David was careful to use the proper order and had the priests carry the ark on their shoulders.

5. **The Appointment of Singers and Musicians** - *"David spake to the chief of the Levites to appoint their brethren to be the singers with instruments of music* (15:16). The importance of the ministry of song with musical instruments in worship is beautifully illustrated. Though they were to play skillfully (see Psalm 33:3), this was not for show, but for worship. Not music by mood or convenience, but appointed singers and musicians, always in their places, worshiping God. Musicians should first be appointed by the leadership, and then trained to flow together in harmony and submission with other musicians, under the anointing of the Holy Spirit, making their music as *"one sound unto the Lord."*

6. **The Placement of Doorkeepers** - (see 15:23,24). Obededom had the ark in his home for three months and he and his family had been so abundantly blessed that he followed the ark to Zion and was made one of the doorkeepers. Let us never underestimate the importance of being a doorkeeper in the house of the Lord. Greeters and ushers in the church are often the first people guests see when they enter

the doors of the church. Their ministry of
love, unity and friendly faith cannot be
over emphasized.

7. **The Appointment of Ministers to Record.**
*"He appointed certain of the Levites to
minister before the ark of the LORD, and
to record, and to thank and praise the
LORD God of Israel* (16:4).They did not
have the convenience of tape recorders,
nevertheless they made recordings of the
prophetic songs at the door of the tent. It
is thought that many of our Psalms were
sung and recorded there. The very first
Psalm was given by David himself and is
recorded in full, beginning with verse 7 of
Chapter 16. The recording of singing and
worship, prophetic ministry and the
preaching of the Word of God is a great
blessing today.

We must not confuse this tent arrangement, later called
"The Tabernacle of David," with "The Tabernacle of
Moses." Moses' Tabernacle was the center of worship in
Israel throughout their wilderness wanderings, and the
reign of Saul. Saul, (a type of the flesh), had no particular
connection with either the Tabernacle of Moses or any
desire to build a temple for God. During his reign, he left
the ark of God in Kirjathjearim (where it remained twenty
years according to 1 Samuel 7:2; 1 Chronicles 13:5).

When David came to the throne, one of his first
questions was, "How can we bring back the ark of God?"
He longed for God's presence, and the cry of his heart
was that the presence of the Lord would be central in his
kingdom.

After the aborted attempt to bring back the ark, David found God's perfect order and the ark was put on the shoulders of the priests (the ministry), not to Shiloh, where Moses' Tabernacle was situated, but to Zion, the City of David. Psalm 78:60, and 68 state that God forsook the Tabernacle in Shiloh, and chose Zion:

> *He forsook the tabernacle of Shiloh, the tent which he placed among men; . . .*
>
> *But chose the tribe of Judah, the mount Zion which he loved.*

If God chose Judah instead of Shiloh, could it be because Judah means praise? Psalm 87:2 says: *"The LORD loveth the gates of Zion more than all the dwellings of Jacob."*

On Mt. Zion, the ark was accessible to all people; there was no veil around it. Everyone could come to the door of the tent and worship freely. This arrangement lasted for many years until the Temple of Solomon was built. If Solomon's Temple is a picture of the reign of Christ in His glory, then the ark in the tent on Zion could be a picture of the new thing God is doing in His church just preceding His coming.

Today, God is making His presence available to all people of all denominations, and many of His people are responding, entering into new dimensions of praise and worship, and learning how to celebrate Jesus.

Amos the prophet referred to this tent on Zion as the "Tabernacle of David." Amos 9:11 states:

> *In that day will I raise up the tabernacle of David that is fallen, and close up the breaches*

thereof; and I will raise up his ruins, and I will build it as in the days of old.

After the ark of the Covenant was removed from the tent which David had prepared and taken into the newly completed Temple of Solomon, there was no further use for the tent. But Amos was looking into the future to a time when God once again would make His glorious presence available to all men everywhere. The ark would no longer be hidden behind a veil in the Temple in Jerusalem, but the presence of the Lord would be in His church, and once again all would worship together around the clock, giving glory to His name.

The apostle James referred to the prophecy of Amos when the church had come together, as recorded in Acts 15, to discuss the Gentiles coming into the church. He compared the church with the rebuilding of the Tabernacle of David where all men might seek after the Lord and where all would have access to His presence.

In this day when God is once again visiting His people, we are witnessing the restoration of the Tabernacle of David. This is why there is so much emphasis on praise and worship. People hunger for this kind of celebration.

This is the time when the Lord is building up Zion, favoring His church with choice truths which have been dormant for years: the five-fold ministry; the gifts of the Spirit; laying on of hands and prophecy; singing praises to the Lord; the new song; local church order; every believer a priest; body ministry; the bonding of beautiful relationships both in local churches and between churches, and a tremendous thrust for world missions.

As we allow Him to build us up, His glory will be revealed in and through His church, and when He completes His work the full revelation of His glory will come.

You can be a part of this praising generation. Here are suggestions to help you enter into what God is doing today.

First, be sure of your relationship with the Lord. Can you say without hesitation, "I am a Christian, I am saved?" The Bible says:

> *If thou shalt confess with thy mouth the Lord Jesus, and shalt believe in thine heart that God hath raised him from the dead, thou shalt be saved.*
>
> (Romans 10:9)

Read it from your Bible. Turn your whole life over to the Lord, trusting in Jesus Christ as your savior, asking God to forgive you and to cleanse you from all sin, and you can know that you are saved. Then say it. "I know I am saved."

Second, ask the Lord to place you in a body of believers, a Bible believing local church, where you will find prayer, the preaching of the Word of God, and celebrant praise and worship. It is impossible to grow in God, just going from church to church as a visitor.

The Bible says in Psalm 92:13,13:

> *Those that be planted in the house of the LORD shall flourish in the courts of our God.*

The way to grow is to be planted. But be sure you are planted in a house of God where people praise, and where prayer is a priority ministry.

Third, move out into the stream of God's blessings and let Him use you. Wonderful things can be happening all around you while you stay in a shell and miss out. Be a participator, not a spectator. Participate. Celebrate! Lift up your hands, lift up your voice, sing unto the Lord. Wait upon Him for prophecy or some other gift of the Spirit.

Fourth, find your ministry in the body. Read Romans 12:6-8 and ask the Lord which of these seven charisma should be flowing through you:

1. Prophecy

2. Serving ministry

3. Teaching

4. Exhorting

5. Giving

6. Ruling

7. Showing mercy

You may naturally be given to one or more of these ministries. Develop them. Bathe them in prayer and praise.

Finally, keep praising. Don't let anything stop you. The devil hates praising people. He had much rather hear you complain or criticize or question. He identifies with that. But when you praise the Lord regardless of circumstances, he becomes confused. Confuse him by celebrating Jesus in new dimensions of praise, and drown out his voice with sounds of celebration.

David won many battles. He was a man after God's own heart, and we think of him as a hero and one to imitate.

The Bible says that we shall be as David. The thing that made David a great man of God was that he was a praiser. He said, *"I will bless the LORD at all times: his praise shall continually be in my mouth"* (Psalm 34:1). He said those words, not in a time of peace, but when he was driven from his own country and was being chased by another king.

Praise God at all times. Offer the sacrifice of praise. Fill His clouds with the vapors of your prayers and praise. Your life will begin to overflow with the rains of His blessings, and you will live in a new kind of victory and joy, and the sounds of celebration will eclipse and drown out all other sounds that try to defeat you, and your whole being can become a perpetual celebration of Jesus!